David Beach
Three Schenkerian-based Studies of Chamber Works
by Mendelssohn, Schumann, and Brahms

Studien und Materialien
zur Musikwissenschaft
Band 121

David Beach
Three Schenkerian-based Studies of Chamber Works
by Mendelssohn, Schumann, and Brahms

Georg Olms Verlag
Hildesheim · Zürich · New York
2022

David Beach

Three Schenkerian-based Studies of Chamber Works
by
Mendelssohn, Schumann, and Brahms

Georg Olms Verlag
Hildesheim · Zürich · New York
2022

The Deutsche Nationalbibliothek lists this publication in the
Deutsche Nationalbibliografie; detailed bibliographic data are available
on the Internet at http://dnb.d-nb.de.

© Georg Olms Verlag AG, Hildesheim 2022
http://www.olms.de
Cover Design: Barbara Gutjahr, Hamburg
Musical graphs were set by Massimo Guida.
Setting: satz&sonders GmbH, Dülmen
Production: Mazowieckie Centrum Poligrafii, Marki
Printed on acid-free and age-resistant paper

Printed in Poland
ISBN 978-3-487-16250-8

Table of Contents

Preface

This thin volume is the product of analytic work accomplished during a year of almost complete isolation from colleagues, friends and relatives forced on us by the global pandemic. Each of us had to deal with this harsh reality in our own way to keep our minds busy and thereby to stave off boredom and potential depression. My solution was to engage in a favorite activity, listening to and studying chamber music of the nineteenth century. I intentionally began my investigation with the music of Felix Mendelssohn, a composer I have always felt is unjustly underrepresented in the analytical literature. I had recently written about the finales from the two piano trios, so I turned to the string quartets, settling on the Sixth, op. 80, in F Minor for my first project. I was attracted to this work not only by the passion of the music but also by the fact that it tells a story. In part it is an outpouring of the composer's grief over the death of his sister, Fanny Hensel, but also, I believe, a tribute to her. This study became the first of the three chapters in this book. Next, I focused on the chamber music of Robert Schumann, settling eventually on his monumental Piano Quintet, op. 44. This is a compelling and engaging work, and, like the Mendelssohn, it projects a narrative, particularly in the final movement, the first half of which I have described as a dialogue among three distinct personalities. Finally, I turned to a successor to the Schumann work, the Piano Quintet in F Minor, op. 34, of Johannes Brahms, one of my absolute favorite works of the nineteenth century. Brahms's references to E Minor in the latter part of the quintet suggest a hidden reference or narrative, but what that may be is not at all clear. Eventually, I decided to present these three studies in this order – Mendelssohn, Schumann, Brahms – that is, in the order in which they were written. There is, in fact, a clear progression across the three studies, each successive work being more complex than the preceding one, offering increasingly greater challenges to the analyst. This arrangement also provides a sense of tonal symmetry, since the Mendelssohn and Brahms works are written in the same key, F Minor, and they share a common important motivic idea, the neighbor-note figure C–D♭–C.

This volume is unique in at least three respects. First, it presents the only complete Schenkerian-based study of these three compositions. It is much more common in general that published articles will deal with a particular movement but not an entire multi-movement work. Second, it contains detailed Schenkerian graphs of all twelve movements, which should be of interest to all those who want to learn more about Schenker's conception of musical structure and its application. Finally, this volume deals in part with repertoire rarely represented in the Schenkerian literature. While Brahms's music deservedly receives a fair amount of attention, Schenkerian analyses of major works by Mendelssohn and Schumann are scarce.

Music analysis is idiosyncratic in nature, a very personal pursuit to discover the inner workings of an individual composition. Sometimes we are rediscovering what others have found before, but for us it is an entirely new and exciting experience. Each of us brings to this process a unique mixture of what we have learned and observed over the years, as well as our acquired analytical biases. No matter how thorough our approach, the result is never as comprehensive as our intent. In this regard, I am often surprised, sometimes pleasantly so, by the observations of others who approached music differently than I. That is, I realize the analyses presented here do not tell us everything that can or should be said about these three works. The analyses are my personal observations and, in some instances, my speculation about the meaning of events. Having said that, I hope all musicians who are attracted to these works will find value in what I have written. Some of my commentary is technical, that is, concerned with matters of voice leading and supported by numerous Schenkerian graphs, but there is also considerable space devoted to issues of formal organization, use of motives and, where appropriate, programmatic matters.

Those well versed in Schenkerian theory and analysis will have little difficulty understanding my graphs and accompanying explanations, but this will be more challenging for those with only a passing acquaintance with this analytical approach. It is certainly beyond the scope of this volume to offer a comprehensive introduction to the topic, but the following walk-through one of the analytic graphs from this book may be of some help. Reproduced below is the initial portion of Example 1-2, a detailed graph of the voice-leading structure of bars 1–61 from the first movement of Mendelssohn's String Quartet in F Minor.

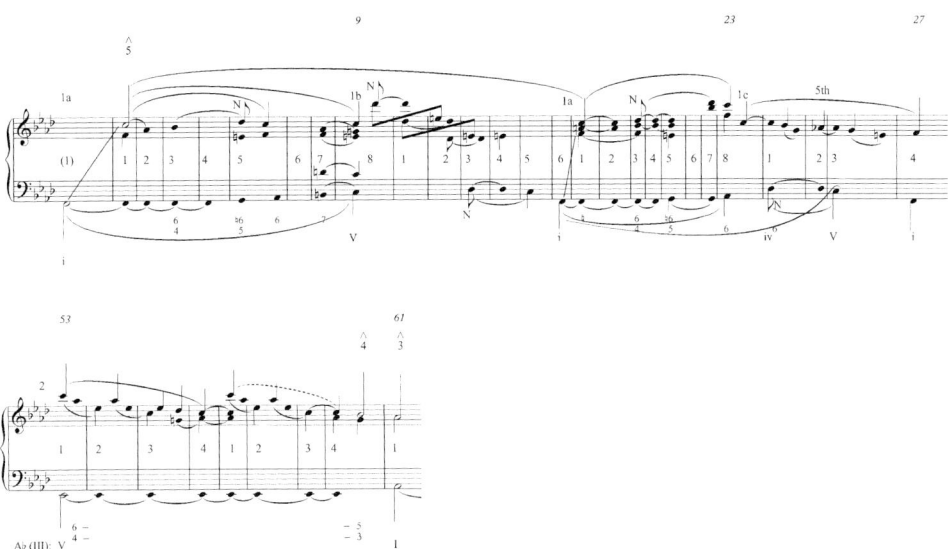

A basic tenet of Schenker's theory is that music consists of multiple levels of structure unfolding simultaneously over the course of a composition, and the intent in analytic graphs is that these levels are clearly reflected in the notation employed. The deepest level of melodic motion and its basic support are notated in this example by half notes, and the melodic pitches at this level are further designated by scale-degree numbers with carets above. This graph shows that the initial melodic tone C ($\hat{5}$) is prolonged at this level until it descends through B♭ to A♭ at the cadence in bars 60–61. More immediate levels of structure are then indicated by quarter notes, eighth notes and finally notes without stems, and slurs are used to delineate levels of prolongation. In this instance the primary tone $\hat{5}$ is initially prolonged in theme 1a by its upper neighbor (notated as an eighth note to indicate that it exists at a lower level than the note it decorates), delineated by a slur, and the continuation shows that this initial pattern is embedded within a replica of this motion from theme 1a across 1b to a varied repetition of 1a, indicated by the larger slur. The primary tone is further prolonged by a descending fifth (theme 1c), then, beginning in bar 53 (theme 2) as an unstable pitch, finally resolving to B♭ and A♭ in conjunction with the modulation to A♭ (III) at bar 61.[1] If you now look ahead to Example 1-4, you can see how this motion is represented in a deeper-level graph.

The three chamber works examined in this volume were written during the mid-nineteenth century, the Brahms somewhat later than the other two, and they share a common musical language, though with clear differences in style. In a certain sense the Mendelssohn stands apart, being the only one of the three written for string quartet, while the Schumann and Brahms invite comparison, being scored for string quartet plus piano. But each of these is a unique work of art, each special in its own way. The common thread throughout this volume is the use of Schenkerian concepts (along with complementary approaches) to reveal at least some of their inner workings, perhaps even some of their secrets.

David Beach
Toronto and Santa Rosa

---

1 The numbers between the staves indicate the hypermetric groupings, which begin with an upbeat measure.

Notational matters

A. Notation of Harmony

You will notice in the ensuing material that I employ a system of indicating major chords with upper-case Roman numerals and minor chords with lower-case ones, though I am well aware that most of my colleagues follow Schenker by indicating all chords with upper-case numerals. I find the system I use to be more flexible and more communicative.

I am also in the habit of indicating an applied or secondary dominant (or dominant substitute, e.g. o7) in square brackets. For example [V] V rather than II♯–V, though on occasion you will encounter II♯ on my graphs.

I indicate augmented sixth chords by +6, e.g. iv^{+6}.

B. Notation of Pitch

I will follow the system employed by the Acoustical Society of America, where middle C is C4.

C. Graphic Notation

It has been my habit for years to provide foreground graphs with bar lines for major portions of a work. (When you encounter an empty bar, it means that the content of that bar is a repetition or a varied repetition of the previous bar.) The advantage of this practice is that the graphs are easy to follow, but the disadvantage is that it is not always possible to show longer-range connections. So my summary examples are middleground / background graphs where greater liberty is taken, for example, in the notation of octave placement to clarify my interpretation of the structure.

Chapter I

Mendelssohn, string quartet no. 6, op. 80, in f minor: In remembrance Fanny Hensel

Felix Mendelssohn began the composition of his final quartet in July-August of 1847 while on retreat in Switzerland, and it was completed in September after his return to Leipzig. Scholars generally agree that this work, the last major work the composer would complete before his death in November, represents the outpouring of Felix's grief over the death of his sister, Fanny Hensel, in May. This loss had such an effect on Felix that he was reported to have temporarily stopped composing, instead finding solace in his paintings, producing several landscapes of the Interlaken area. Eventually he would return to composition to find a way to express his grief in music, the result being the op. 80 quartet. The Mendelssohn scholar, R. Larry Todd, provides the following general description.

> The string quartet in F Minor, op. 80, drafted during the final Swiss sojourn and cast in the composer's most dissonant, disjunct style, is laden with grief over Fanny… The outer movements are in an unrelenting, dynamic, agitated style, with driving tremolos, wide leaps, and forays into the high register. The tender slow movement, placed as the penultimate third movement, seems to reminisce about the intimate, lyrical style of Fanny's lieder, while the second movement, propelled by jarring syncopations, is a macabre scherzo such as Felix imagined his sister might have composed. [1,2]

The quartet is unified by a recurring motive C–D♭–C that pervades different levels of the structure, the one exception being the third movement, which offers a semblance of a respite from the general tone of the work. As we shall see, the quartet is also unified by an underlying narrative pertaining to Fanny, as suggested by the subtitle of this chapter. That is, this work is more closely connected to Fanny than just an outpouring of Felix's grief. It has already been noted that the second movement represents the composer's imagination of how his sister might have written it. Though we will touch on programmatic matters several times in the following pages, consider for a moment the two sudden digressions in the exposition of the first movement (bars 73–76 and 82–85), which ever-so-briefly suggest ♭II and ♭VI, respectively, in the local key. What is their meaning? From a structural perspective they are parenthetical digressions, delaying the progress of the tonal motion to the dominant of A♭ (III). But that hardly explains why they are there and what they represent. They are intrusions, sudden recollections of his sister or happier times past,

---

1 As stated by the composer in a letter to Sebastian Hensel. See *Felix Mendelssohn: A Life in Letters*, ed. R. Elvers, trans. C. Tomlinson, 381.

2 Todd, *Fanny Hensel: The Other Mendelssohn*, 350–51.

much like what happens to all of us when a sudden recollection intrudes on our thought process.

Mendelssohn's treatment of sonata form in this work represents a break from his earlier quartets, which are decidedly "classical" in their design. We could debate at great length whether or not there is a classical model for sonata form, but we all have a basic plan in mind against which we measure variants. Mendelssohn's earlier works, for example the first movement of the third quartet, op. 44, no. 1, is a clear example of the procedures inherent in this model, but the outer movements of op. 80 deviate from it in several respects, e.g., the overlapping of major sections and the reversal of order of presentation of thematic material in the recapitulation. This raises the matter of terminology to be employed here. Terminology can be confusing. For example, most formalists identify the recapitulation as beginning with the return of the main theme, no matter in what key, while Schenkerians normally identify the recapitulation commencing with the return to the tonic. The confusion arises from the use of the same term to describe, on the one hand, a formal event, and, on the other, a tonal event. We can avoid the confusion by referring to the formal return and the tonal return if the situation requires it. Often they occur simultaneously (the classical model), but there are wonderful examples where they do not.

The following discussion of each movement is divided into two parts, the first dealing with form and related matters, including the narrative, and the second focusing more on voice leading and structural issues.

I. Allegro vivace assai

An outline of the formal-tonal design of the movement is provided in Table 1-1. This chart identifies three components of the first theme area. The first of these (1a) is the tremolo phrase that establishes not only the general tone of the movement but also the key and primary tone ($\hat{5}$). This phrase has the character of an introduction, but as the movement progresses it becomes clear that it is an integral component of the discourse. The 1b idea that follows is characterized by the leap of a diminished seventh from D♭, the pervasive upper neighbor of the primary tone, down to E♮. This harmony (o7) appears frequently at important junctures in this movement as a substitute for the dominant. This is followed by a varied restatement of the initial tremolo phrase, creating a mini a–b–a' structure that leads to a third idea (1c) of an entirely different character from the preceding agitated material. It is interesting that this new lyrical idea is derived rhythmically from 1b, as shown in Example 1-1. It is a four-bar idea that is repeated in varied form twice, the second time extended to lead to the dominant of A♭ (III).

The second theme – a clear contrast to the agitated character of the 1a and 1b ideas – is notable in two respects: first, the bass of the entire phrase is a dominant pedal until the resolution to the perfect authentic cadence in the new key at bar 61; and second, the "melodic" line above consists primarily of arpeggios extending the six-four until its reso-

TABLE 1-1. MENDELSSOHN (I): CHART OF FORMAL/TONAL DESIGN

EXPOSITION

Theme 1		
1a	1–9	f: i–V
1b	9–15	o7
1a′	15–23	i–i6
1c and cont.	23–41	i6–iv–V–i
Trans.	41–53	i → V7 of III
Theme 2		
init. statement	53–61	A♭: V–I
rep. and cont.	61–86	I–ii–V
Closing idea	86–95	→ V7

DEVELOPMENT

1a	96–110	→ V7 of c minor (v)
1b dev.	110–118	c: o7–i6
	118–141	C7–A7–D–g6–f6–E♭
	141–161	e♭ … G♭
Retrans.(1a)	161–172	f: o7

RECAPITULATION

Theme 1c	172–190	f: i6–V–i
Trans.	190–212	i–V
Theme 2 and cont.	213–240	F: I
Closing idea	241–252	I–V7
Bridge (1a)	252–258	f: o7
Theme 1a	259–266	i–iv
Theme 1b	266–290	V–i
Coda [Presto]	290–323	I–ii–V–i

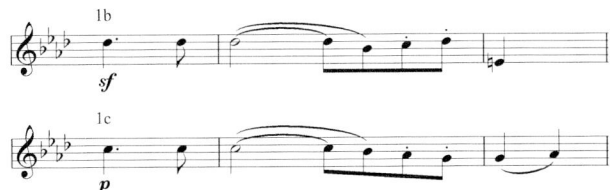

Example 1-1. Mendelssohn (I): Comparison of themes 1b and 1c

lution to five-three in the penultimate bar. The significance of this idea to our narrative will become apparent when it appears in the recapitulation. Here, in the continuation of this idea, elements of the minor mode, first F♭, then later C♭, creep into the dialogue, darkening the brighter mood. It is into this context that the two brief disruptions referred to earlier, which may very well represent sudden recollections of Fanny, are inserted into the discourse. The second of these leads to a closing idea, beginning in bar 86, that returns us to the lyricism and relative calm reminiscent of the 1c idea. Still there is a sense of urgency created by the increased insistence on V7 in the key of A♭ with its prominent D♭. In fact, the exposition ends suddenly with this harmony, interrupted abruptly by the intrusion of the opening tremolo idea and the negative sense it conveys. From a theoretical perspective we must concern ourselves with the eventual resolution of the dissonant D♭. Equally important we must consider the meaning of the abrupt abandonment of this dissonance. Had Felix wanted to pose a rhetorical "why?", for example, he might have followed the hanging dissonance by a grand pause. Rather the point seems to be the intrusion of dark thoughts into the calm offered by this repetitive lilting tune.

The sudden intrusion of the tremolo idea signals the beginning of the development section, the remainder of which is based almost entirely on the contrapuntal treatment of the 1b idea with its characteristic dotted rhythm and descending wide leap. The initial phrase of this passage (bars 110–118) is divided into two parts: imitative statements of the 1b motive (4 bars, o7 of v) and four bars extending the resolution of the o7 to a C minor harmony in first inversion. The repetition of this phrase begins from a C7 chord (V7), but the continuation leads through a number of chords, arriving eventually at an E♭ chord in bar 141 to initiate a passage leading to the climax of the movement at the high B♭ and the o7 chord at bar 161.[3] Here the return of the tremolo idea functions locally as a retransition, not as the beginning of the recapitulation, with the characteristic o7 substituting for the dominant, one result of which is the restatement of the D♭ left unresolved at the very end of the exposition. A secondary advantage of the o7 is that it allows Mendelssohn to slide almost unnoticed into the recapitulation (second half of bar 172) with a statement of the 1c idea, which begins from a weak position of the tonic harmony. The effect of this is a

---

3 Mendelssohn returns to this high B♭ (*ff*) in the coda (bar 317) just prior to the final cadence.

subtle overlapping of sections.[4] There is not a strong return to tonic harmony until the perfect authentic cadence at bar 190.

Following the cadence in bar 190, there is a transitional passage leading to theme 2, this time in F major. This is the focal point of the recapitulation, and now we can grasp the significance of Mendelssohn's choice of F Minor/Major for this work as well as the characteristics of the theme itself with its pedal point on F and melodic emphasis on A. It is a tribute to his sister: FAnny. This time the continuation to the closing phrase contains only one, not two disruptions. This closing idea leads us back to F minor and subsequent statements of themes 1a and 1b followed by a *presto* coda (bars 290–323).[5] There can be various reasons for Mendelssohn's choice to save statements of 1a and 1b for the end of the movement. From a purely practical perspective their statement earlier following a development largely devoted to 1b and a retransition based on 1a might not have been appropriate. Whatever the reason, the result is that the focus falls first on the tribute to Fanny while the movement closes with the strong statements expressing his grief.

An interpretation of the voice-leading structure of this movement is offered in Examples 1-2 to 1-5. With the exception of Example 1-4, these are foreground graphs with bar lines included for ease in following the interpretation, and on occasion a group of bars are left blank, indicating that the content is a varied repetition of the preceding material. Also, there are places where entire passages have been omitted if the content is not necessary to follow the longer-range connections. Finally, you will note that the hypermetric organization, which is predominantly quadruple, is indicated between the staves, and brackets are employed to indicate parenthetical phrase insertions.

Example 1-2 is a graph of the exposition. The initial phrase establishes the primary tone C5 ($\hat{5}$), which is prolonged locally by its upper neighbor D♭ and then D♮ at the final approach to the cadence on V.[6] This phrase is preceded by an upbeat measure, which is notated as (1) in the hypermeter to indicate the potential for hearing this and the following bar as successive downbeat measures, a feature that emerges later in the movement. The following 1b idea features D♭, the upper neighbor of $\hat{5}$, in several octaves, most notably in the upper octave, which is picked up in the final bars of the next phrase, the varied statement of the tremolo idea (1a). This is followed by the initial statement of 1c, the main feature of which is the descending fifth from C5. Repetitions of this idea, the second of which is expanded by an internal insertion delaying arrival at the cadence, are not shown in

---

4 A different interpretation of this passage is given by Erez Rapoport in *The Smoothing Over of Formal Junctures as a Style Element in Mendelssohn's Instrumental Music*, Ex. 3.20 (p. 176). Curiously Rapoport identifies the beginning of the recapitulation at bar 167, which falls within a prolonged dominant/o7 chord.

5 An earlier example that comes to mind where the statement of ideas is reversed in the recapitulation is Schubert's *Quartettsatz*, D. 703, of 1820.

6 A note about notation: Since the primary emphasis on C5 falls at the cadence, it might make sense to notate the establishment of $\hat{5}$ over V at the cadence rather than earlier, as indicated in Example 1-2.

Example 1-2. Regarding the motive C–D♭–C, it is represented here in different octaves and both locally and across longer spans. Note the expression of this idea in the bass, supporting the harmonic progression iv6–V, for example in bars 24–26, as well as in the top voice.

As noted in the preceding discussion of form, the main features of the second theme are the bass pedal point on E♭, the dominant of A♭ (III), above which the top part descends, primarily through arpeggiation, from C6. The repetition of the four-bar idea eventually resolves the six-four to five-three in the lower octave, leading the fundamental line through B♭4 ($\hat{4}$) to A♭4 ($\hat{3}$) at the cadence on A♭. This structural feature – the motion of the fundamental line to $\hat{3}$ at the cadence within the second key area – is a common paradigm with sonata movements in the minor mode. The most important feature of the continuation is the reintroduction of D♭5, first in bar 71, then later in bars 86–87 following the two interruptive insertions. Not shown is the following closing idea, which stresses this pitch. The fact that Mendelssohn chooses to end the exposition abruptly with this dissonant seventh, rudely interrupted by the tremolo idea, is certainly noteworthy. This dissonance demands resolution, but we will have to wait for some time for this to be resolved satisfactorily.

Example 1-3 is a graph of the development section as related to the final gesture of the exposition and the initial statement of 1c at the beginning of the recapitulation. The initial voice leading involves the process of reaching over or overlapping, where the resolutions of dissonant sevenths are clearly implied, though not explicitly stated, at least in the same voice or octave. These resolutions are supplied in parentheses. So the dissonant D♭5 at the end of the exposition resolves in the immediate context to an implied C5 over the o7 of ii harmony in the local key (bar 101), above which E♭5 is introduced, which resolves to an implied D♭ over a B♭ (bar 104), above which F5 is introduced… In this case F6, the dissonant seventh of the G7 chord (V7 of C Minor), is resolved – after the introduction of the 1b idea – following its transfer to the bass. This process then continues until B♭6 is reached, first associated with an E♭ harmony, then three measures later with a B♭ chord (iv), which is prolonged over the following eight measures before the bass argeggiates through ♭II to the diminished seventh chord at the beginning of the retransition (bar 161). At two important junctures along the way (bars 112–113 and 141–142) there are successive downbeat measures in the hypermetric structure. In addition, note the existence of conflicting hypermetric groups in bars 129–142, the prevailing pattern below and the conflicting one (violin 1) above, a conflict that is finally resolved at bar 142. Returning now to the retransition, it prolongs the o7 chord as substitute for the dominant. This allows Mendelssohn to reintroduce the dissonant D♭ and to progress almost unnoticed to a statement of 1c, which, at least in retrospect, signals a return – a weak return – to the tonic.

Example 1-4 provides an overview of the movement to the tonic return. The first theme in the exposition is shown to descend a fifth prolonging C5 ($\hat{5}$), and the second theme leads the primary line through B♭4 ($\hat{4}$) to A♭4 ($\hat{3}$) at the cadence on III. Our expectation is that this will lead eventually to $\hat{2}$ /V in the retransition. The exposition then ends with V7 in the key of A♭. The graph of the development section omits the initial steps in the

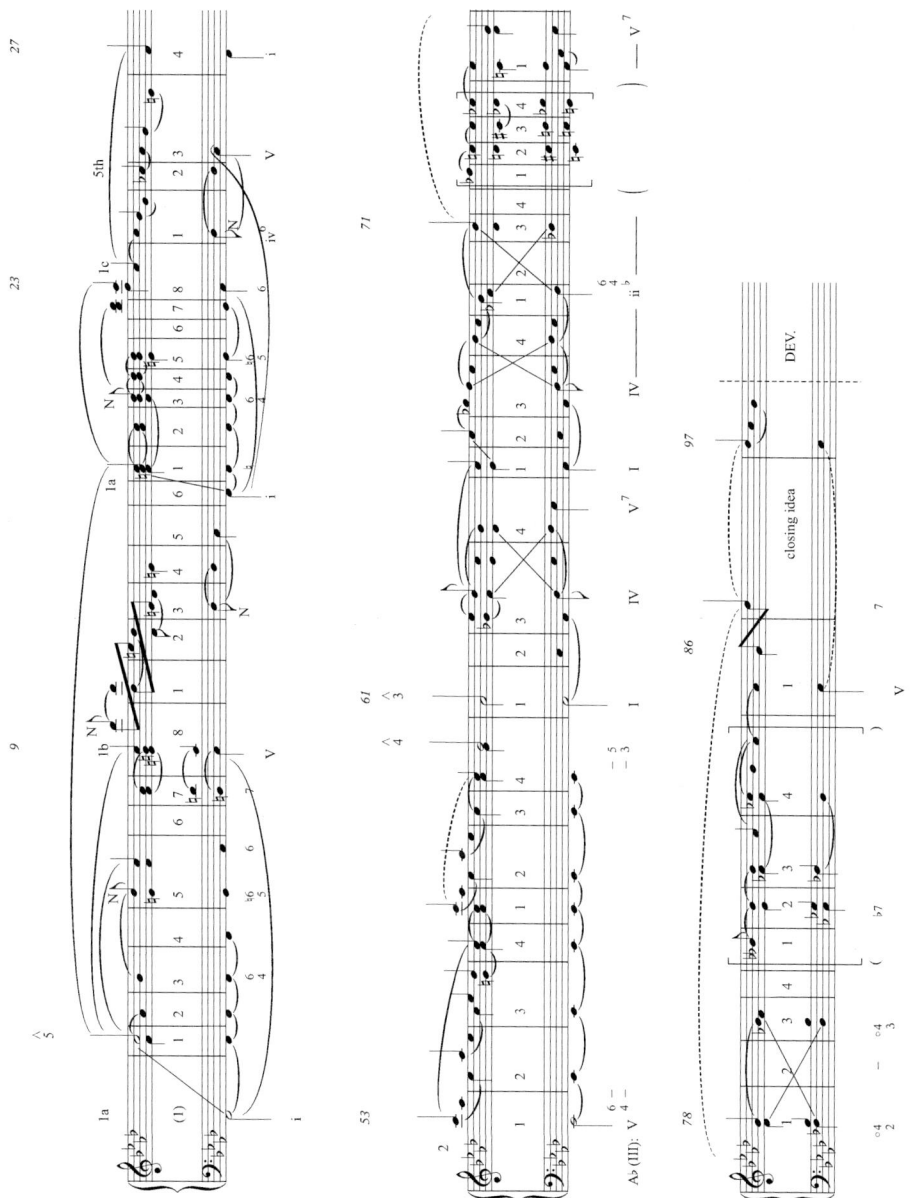

Example 1-2. Mendelssohn (I): Foreground graph of the exposition

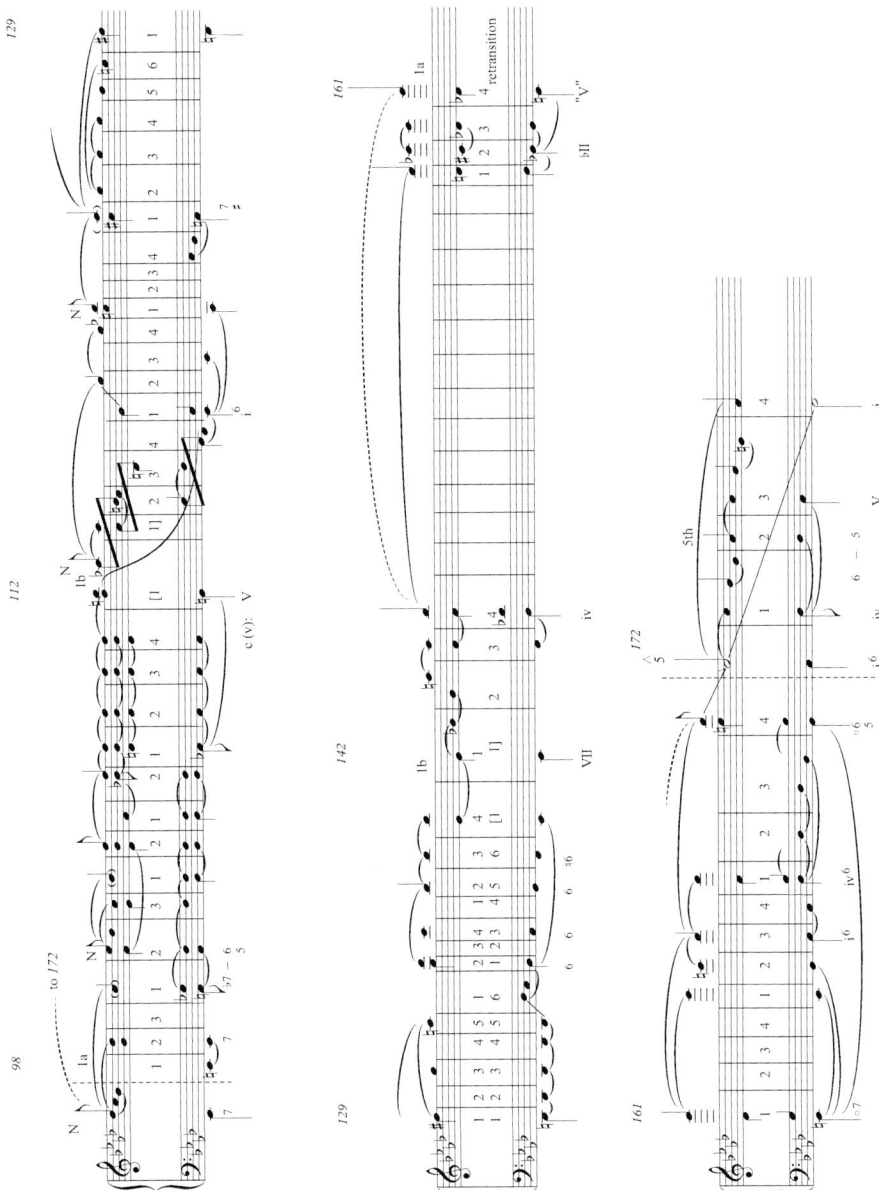

Example 1-3. Mendelssohn (I): Foreground graph of the development and beginning of the recapitulation

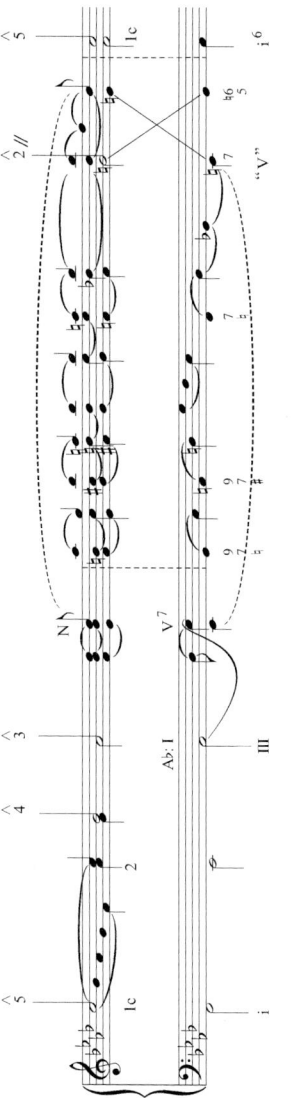

Example 1-4. Mendelssohn (I): Middleground graph of the exposition and development

overlapping process noted above, but instead focusses on the ascent to the covering B♭5, which is extended briefly to B♭6 in the music. The continuation of the fundamental line to $\hat{2}$ is shown to exist in an inner voice supported by the °7 chord. This is a reasonable assertion, though the main focus here is not on this aspect of the structure, but on the return to D♭5 and its resolution to C5 at the beginning of the recapitulation. The extended dotted line above the graph posits a connection between D♭5 at the end of the exposition to the D♭5 at the very end of the retransition above a chromatic change in the bass from E♭ to E♮, in short a gigantic expansion of the *Ur*-motive.

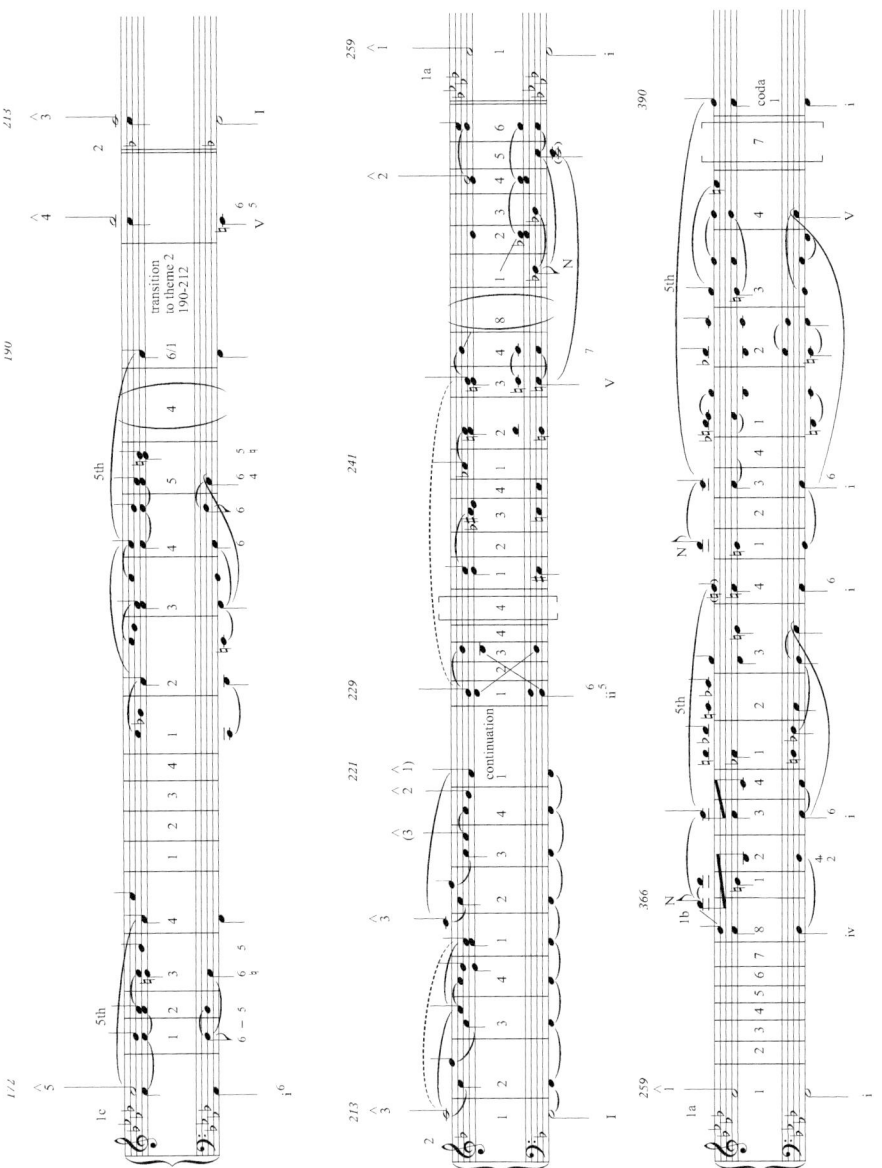

Example 1-5. Mendelssohn (I): Foreground graph of the recapitulation

Example 1-5 is a graph of large portions of the recapitulation, omitting some passages not crucial to an understanding of the overall structure. The initial statement of 1c, which is repeated twice in varied form, descends a fifth from the primary tone C5. The continuation / transition (not shown in Example 1-5) leads to a clear articulation of B♭5 ($\hat{4}$), supported by the dominant, which leads immediately to A5 ($\natural\hat{3}$) at the beginning of theme 2. Mendelssohn has been very careful to prepare the approach to this crucial spot, where he highlights the first two letters in Fanny's name in pitches. This second idea then continues the descent to closure but at a more immediate structural level than the preceding $\hat{4}$ and $\hat{3}$, as indicated by the notation in the graph. It is in the continuation that the music begins to settle convincingly on G4 ($\hat{2}$), first supported by the supertonic in bars 229–232, then by V7 in bars 243–244, though covered by the seventh, then again in bar 256 (where the covering seventh is transferred to an inner voice) before continuing on to structural closure on the downbeat of bar 259. Note the reference to the D♭–C motive in the bass here, which Mendelssohn aborts at the last minute by substituting E♮ for the expected C. It is interesting that Mendelssohn has avoided strong root motion at places where it is normally expected, for example at the approach to the recapitulation and here at the point of structural closure, which contributes to the underlying sense of uncertainty, perhaps even anxiety, this movement conveys. The graph posits tonal closure before the statements of 1a and 1b and the concurrent return to the minor mode. These statements of the opening agitated ideas refer once again to the D♭–C motive and to the descending fifth, now in the upper octave. But these are not part of the fundament structure, but rather summary statements of the main features of the movement.

II. Allegro assai

This scherzo movement is one of extreme contrasts, at one moment very serious, but suddenly light-hearted and playful. Perhaps this characteristic is something Felix perceived in his sister's music, but the angst-filled main idea with its driving syncopations is certainly by Felix. Another possible link to Fanny is their shared interest in earlier music, especially Bach, represented in this movement by the employment of a ground bass in the trio. These and other possible links to Fanny's musical interests and her compositional style are speculative, of course, arising from Felix's comment that he wanted to write a scherzo movement as he imagined his sister would have written it.

Table 1-2 is an outline of the formal-tonal plan of this engaging movement. In its overall design, the form is ternary, as is the design of each of its sections. As is common, the first statement of the scherzo is cast in a rounded binary format ||: a :||: b a′ :||. The initial phrase of the scherzo, where we hear once again the C–D♭–C idea that pervades the quartet, is characterized by its strong forward momentum (repeated syncopated pattern) and loud dynamic until arrival at the cadential pattern beginning in bar 12, where the character suddenly becomes light and playful. This sixteen-bar phrase is then repeated. The

TABLE 1-2. MENDELSSOHN (II): CHART OF FORMAL-TONAL DESIGN

A′. SCHERZO

a	1–16	f: V6 .... iv–V–i
bridge (based on a)	17–24	c(v): V7
b		
octave passage	25–28, 29–32	i
contrapuntal cont.	33–43	i–iv–V7
retransition	43–50	f: II7–(i) –
a′	51–86a	V6 .... iv–V ( ) i

B. TRIO

ground bass (based on b)	86b–101	f: i–[V] III
a bass and ctpt.	102–117	i–[V7] III
"b"	118–141	F7–G7–o7
a′	142–161	I–[V7] III
retransition	162–178	o7

A′. SCHERZO

a	179–194	f: V6 ....iv–V–i
bridge	195–202	c(v): V7
b		
octave passage	203–06, 207–10	i
contrapuntal cont.	211–221	i–iv–V7
retransition	221–228	f. II7–i –
a′	229–263	V6 .... iv–V–i
CODA (based on the trio)	264–301	i–iv–i

following bridge, which continues the syncopated idea of the a section, is based on a single chord, V7 in the key of the dominant, C Minor. This leads to a passage in open octaves, a four-bar idea that is repeated, and the continuation, set contrapuntally in contrast, leads again to V7 in C Minor.[7] The extension / retransition leads to a repeat of the a phrase, this time extended internally by a twenty-bar insertion delaying arrival at the final tonic. An interesting feature of this retransition is the inclusion of four bars of tonic harmony immediately before the return to a′, that is, between V7 of V and V6, the initial chord of a′. This not only anticipates the return to C, the main melodic note, but shifts the emphasis back – if only in passing – to F Minor.

---

7 This ten-bar phrase includes a six-bar group, the only non-quadruple metric group in the movement.

The trio opens with a sixteen-bar ground bass stated in octaves (viola and cello) that is divided into eight plus eight bars with the first eight divided into four plus its varied repetition. As shown in Table 1-2, the harmony of this phrase progresses from tonic to mediant. In the following sixteen bars the violins are added in counterpoint to the repeated bass pattern, progressing primarily in parallel sixths. The following b phrase is unsettled harmonically, progressing from F7 to G7 to the diminished seventh chord to reintroduce a variant of the a phrase, which is extended by repetition of the final four bars. The retransition, which prolongs D♭ is notable in two respects. First is the interchange between o7 and E♭7, two chords that have played important roles within the trio, but their appearance here also potentially refers to their roles in the first movement, again as support for D♭. You might recall that the exposition of the first movement ended abruptly with the E♭7 chord, and later it is this diminished seventh chord that replaced the dominant in the retransition. Second the transfer of the third D♭–B♭ to the upper octave and the acceleration of its repetition anticipates and prepares the return to the scherzo. As noted on the Table, the coda is based on material from the trio, both the bass and the counterpoint above.

A middleground graph of the scherzo is provided in Example 1-6. Following immediately after the first movement, the most notable feature of the opening of the scherzo from a voice-leading perspective is the emphasis on C5 and its prolongation by its upper neighbor D♭. C5 is marked as the potential primary tone, though there is no descent from $\hat{5}$ within this movement; rather C5 seems to hover above a descent from A♭ in an inner voice. The voice leading of this phrase employs the technique of reaching over, similar to what we encountered in the development section of the first movement. Here the opening C5 gives way to B♭4 to begin this process. This B♭4 reaches up to D♭5 to approach C5 from above, then this C5 reaches up to E♭5 to introduce D♭5, the upper neighbor, which returns to C5 at the cadence. In the b section the G7 harmony of the bridge leads to a C Minor chord (v) in bar 25 (initiating the passage in open octaves), which is restated at bar 33. The following passage, the contrapuntal continuation and the retransition leading to the first chord of a′, prolongs the dominant, transforming it from minor to major as indicated by the diagonal line in Example 1-6 from the inner voice E♭4 (bar 33) to the bass E♮ (bar 51). (This connection is obscured somewhat by the four-bar emphasis on the tonic harmony immediately prior to the return to a and dominant harmony.) The a phrase is then repeated with the afore-mentioned internal expansion delaying the final cadence.

Providing a graph of the trio is a bit more difficult due to the length and repetition of the ground bass, which is not shown separately in Example 1-7. The counterpoint above the ground bass in the a phrase is shown in this example to descend a sixth from A♭4 to C4, broken into two thirds. Then, in the b phrase, a secondary melodic idea is created by the ascending leaps to C5, then D♮5, a welcome relief from the restricted range of the preceding material. The return to C5, the completion of the C-D-C idea, comes after the return to the a phrase, creating an overlap across the phrase division. Again, the upper line descends a sixth from A♭4 to C4, followed by the introduction of the upper neighbor D♭4–D♭5.

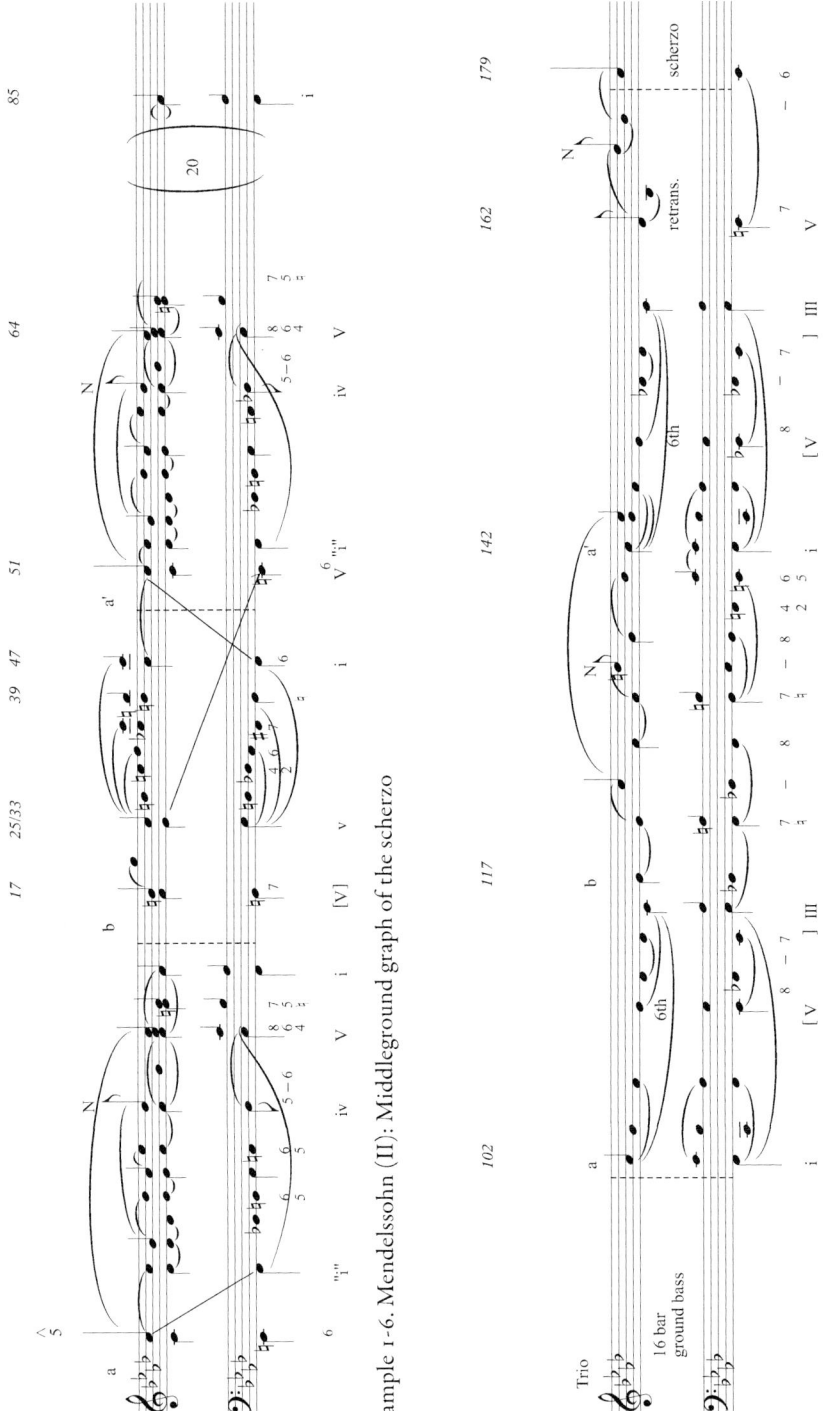

Example 1-6. Mendelssohn (II): Middleground graph of the scherzo

Example 1-7. Mendelssohn (II): Middleground graph of the trio

Typical of a trio, the melodic material is repetitive and the range largely restricted to an octave. The relative stasis of the trio makes the return of the initial phrase of the scherzo with its driving energy all the more effective.

III. Adagio

In some respects this movement can be taken as a relief from the turbulence of the remainder of the quartet. Indeed, there are occasional moments where the music comes to momentary rest, e.g., the cadences at bars 17, 39, 94 and at the very end, but throughout there is an undercurrent of restlessness and anxiety, even anguish, that pervades the movement from the very beginning. Consider the opening idea. The initial melodic gesture (violin 1), the descending leap of a minor sixth A^b5–$C5$ (an anguished sigh?), is stated over an F minor harmony (vi), not the tonic, a reference, it would seem, to the overall tonic of the quartet, and this leads to a 7-6 suspension over D^b, and it is not until the supertonic harmony is led on to V7 and I that our disorientation is dissipated. But even here, with the arrival at the tonic, there is no relaxation due to the dovetailed entrance of the opening idea in the violin 2 part. This statement leads us to a brief cadence on the dominant (bar 8) and a contrasting phrase that returns to a statement of the opening idea, this time progressing to a cadence on the tonic (downbeat of bar 17).[8] To summarize, this A section has a formal design of a a b a', ending with a perfect authentic cadence. But once again the music does not come to rest for very long, as the point of arrival becomes the point of departure for the next section.

The B section opens with dovetailed statements of a four-bar idea: violin 1 – violin 2 – viola – violin 1, where the fourth bar becomes the first bar of the overlapping statement: 1 2 3 4/1, etc. With the fourth statement there begins a process of dissolution of the motive with repetitions of what had been the rhythm of the third bar of the original idea. It appears as if Mendelssohn might have been headed toward a cadence in bar 32, but he avoids this, and the music pushes through to a cadence on the dominant in bar 39. Meanwhile the process of dissolution has continued, culminating in repetitions at the half measure, most notably the repeated $G4$–$F4$–E^b4 third of bars 34–35, which sound like a repeated sigh.[9] Arrival at the cadence in bar 39 is then extended, featuring a dotted rhythmic figure recalling the opening violin gesture of the movement. This extension introduces the seventh of the dominant in the upper octave in preparation for the return to $C5$. It is not until the entrance of the descending sixth in the violin 1 part (upbeat to bar 50) that we realize Mendelssohn has slipped into the return of A material almost unnoticed.

---

8 Mendelssohn prepares the return very carefully with the statements of the descending fourth A^b–G–F–E^b in two registers anticipating the cello A^b–G–F–E–F.

9 This insistent gesture is repeated later a fourth higher in bars 89–90 at the approach to the cadence in bar 94.

The A′ section begins as we might expect with statements of the a, a′ and b phrases, and it is not surprising that Mendelssohn would choose to expand the final phrase. What is unexpected is the length of this expansion into what is an extended digression, a mini development section, that delays arrival at the cadence until bar 94. This digression develops ideas from both sections, first from A and then from B, and it leads chromatically / enharmonically into a distant dreamland far from home. It is fascinating that what pulls us back to reality is the harmony in bars 80–82 above D♭ (minor subdominant), which leads to a varied repetition of bars 28–39 a fifth lower to lead to the cadence on A♭. This cadence is then extended parallel to the earlier extension of the cadence on V, and, like the earlier extension, it becomes a transition to a restatement of the opening idea. The final statement of the plaintive "theme", beginning with the unaccompanied cello, leads this time to a peaceful, almost wistful resolution.[10]

A foreground graph of the A section (bars 1–17) is given in Example 1-8. The primary tone is identified as C5, the primary tone of all four movements, here $\hat{3}$ in the key of A♭. Identification of the tonic harmony from the very beginning is a product of hindsight, since, in reality, the tonic is not stated explicitly until the end of the first phrase. In this first phrase C5 is prolonged by its upper neighbor D♭, by now a very familiar sound in this quartet. The second phrase, which progresses to the dominant leads the top part to the covering tone E♭5, which becomes an important feature of the B section. The third phrase (b) then leads back to a statement of the opening cello idea and reintroduction of the primary tone via the descending third E♭5–D♭5–C5. Extension of the passing tone D♭5 within this third and its supporting harmony (ii) result in the extension of the phrase from 4 to 5 bars. The final phrase then leads to local closure in bar 17 with the covering tone E♭5 hovering above.

Example 1-9 is a middleground graph of the B and A′ sections (bars 17–94).[11] Following the overlapping statements of the four-bar idea in the opening bars of the B section, the top voice progresses to the covering tone E♭5 supported by dominant harmony, and eventually the music leads to the rather unique cadential progression in bars 36–39, in which the standard progression is expanded to accommodate the descent of an entire fifth from B♭4 to E♭4. The unusual feature is the embedded harmonization of the second step (the A♭) within the descending fifth. Overall the deep structure of A and B combined is an interruption of the fundamental structure, $\hat{3}$/I – $\hat{2}$/V, above which D♭5 is introduced in the subsequent extension of the cadence on V to lead the covering E♭5 back to the primary tone C5 and tonic harmony at bar 50 (A′). The initial portion of the A′ section progresses once again from the primary tone through D5 to the covering tone E♭5 at bar 56, and it is the following phrase that leads us to the supertonic harmony (bar 58) and the ensuing enharmonic digression.

---

10 I decided not to present a chart of the formal-tonal design of this movement, mainly because I thought this verbal description would capture the essence of the movement more accurately.

11 A graph of the final portion of the movement following structural closure at bar 94 has not been provided.

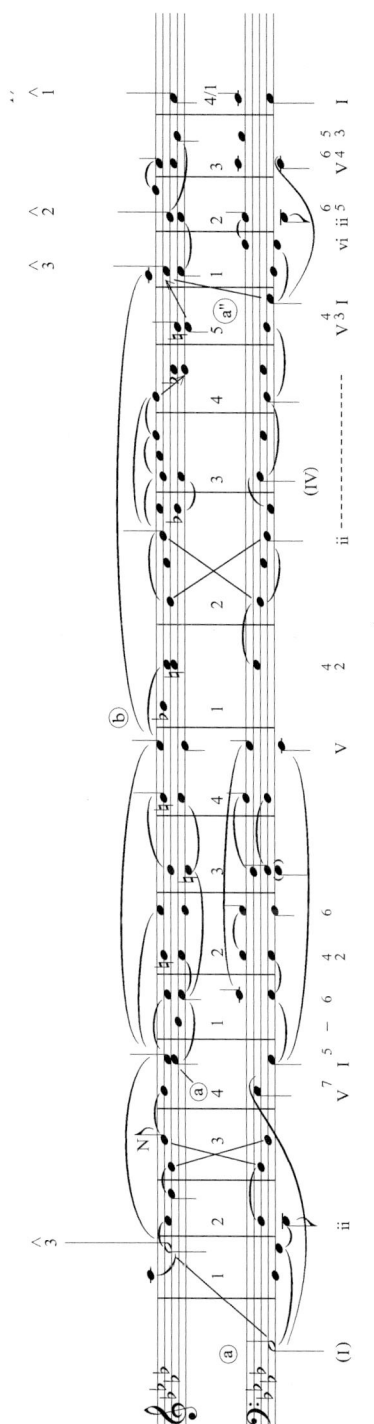

Example 1-8. Mendelssohn (III): Foreground graph of the A section

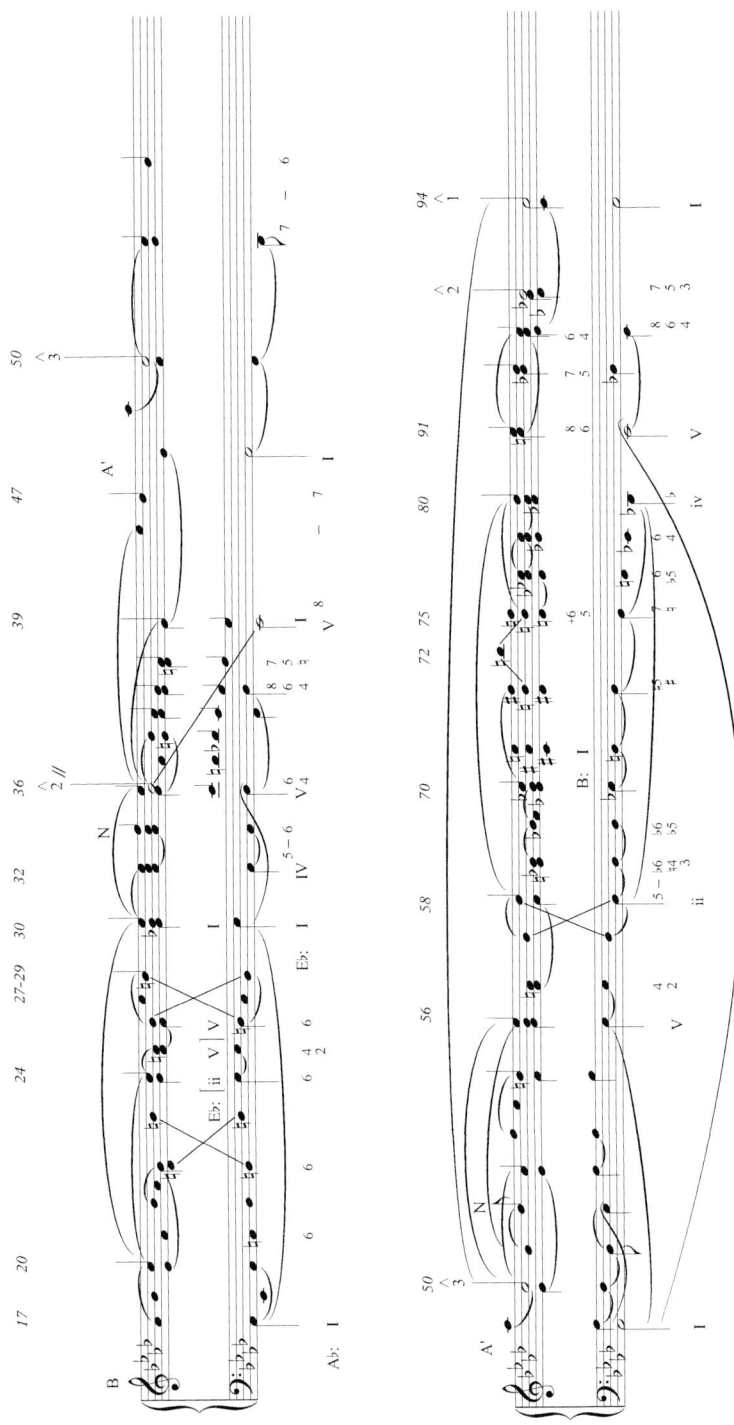

Example 1-9. Mendelssohn (III): Middleground graph of the B and A' sections

This digression becomes increasingly dissonant and agitated before settling on its immediate goal, C♭/B major, which is internal to the larger connection between bar 58 and minor subdominant (bar 80) shown in Example 1-9. Arrival at bar 80 then leads to a repetition of the expanded cadential progression of bars 36–39, now a fourth higher to close on î. It is worthy of note that this digression prolongs D♭5, which plays such an important role throughout this quartet, but also that the goal of this digression is the minor subdominant. As noted above, this is a very serious movement, full of angst and deep emotional feeling. It is this third movement more than the others that seems to be the real tribute to Fanny as well as the most heart-felt outpouring of the composer's deep sorrow.

IV. Finale – allegro molto

This powerful finale contains numerous references to the first movement, most notably the motive C–D♭–C, but other features as well, which will be noted in the following discussion of the movement's formal-tonal design, outlined in Table 1-3.[12] The first theme, characterized by its Lombard rhythm and stated almost entirely over a tonic pedal, much like the second theme in the first movement, is eight bars in length, leading from i to V. The extension, also eight bars in length, recalls the tremolos that opened the quartet. The second statement ends on a D♭ chord, the subdominant in the key of A♭ (III), and the following transition prolongs D♭5, harmonized as the seventh of the dominant in that key. Except for the tremolos in bars 9–13, this is the first significant reference to the motive C–D♭–C, where C is once again the primary tone ($\hat{5}$). The following second "theme" is a four-bar idea that is treated imitatively, similar in some respects to the treatment of the four-bar idea at the beginning of the B section in the preceding movement, though extended here for thirty-two bars. It ends with an E♭7 chord (V7 in A♭), leaving the D♭ momentarily unresolved and bringing this short exposition to an abrupt halt, a very clear reference to the equivalent place in the first movement.

The development section is based entirely on the first theme and its characteristic rhythm; it can be divided into three subsections followed by a retransition, which is extended by a lengthy digression. The first part consists of a statement of the theme in F♭ major (♭VI in A♭), and the extension leads briefly to A♭ Minor, followed by a passage based on a rhythmic fragment of the theme that returns to A♭ Major and the primary tone C5 via V7 and D♭5. The second part, again based on a fragment of the theme, enters forcefully (*ff*), and this idea is then treated sequentially: [V7] iv [V7] v in the original key. This leads to the third part, commencing in bar 161, that begins on the subdominant and leads eventually to

---

12 This and other similar outlines are presented with the caveat that such charts in general are imperfect reflections of a movement's contents and that there are places where formal boundaries are not entirely clear. I suspect, for example, that there might be some disagreement about where the coda begins, but in general I believe this outline is an accurate reflection of this aspect of the movement's organization.

TABLE 1-3. MENDELSSOHN (IV): CHART OF FORMAL-TONAL DESIGN

EXPOSITION

Theme 1

statement 1			
	theme	2–9	f: i–V
	extension (tremolos)	10–17	V
statement 2			
	theme	18–29	i–V, [ii7–V] VI
	extension / trans.	30–48	A♭: IV–V7
Theme 2 and extension		49–80	A♭ (III): vi … V7

DEVELOPMENT

Part 1

theme 1	81–89	A♭ :♭VI
extension	89–96	♭VI
repeated fragment (theme 1)	97–124	V7–I

Part 2

statement 1, theme 1 fragment	125–140	f: [V7] iv
statement 2	141–160	[V7] v6 [V6/5] i6 [V6/5] iv6

Part 3

theme 1	161–180	iv6 … V7 of V

Retransition

dominant	181–212	V
digression (new theme)	213–228	VI
	229–268	VII–i–iv6–V

RECAPITULATION

Theme 1 and extension	269–288	i–V
Theme 2	289–305	VI–V–i
	305–324	i–iv6–V
Theme 1 and ext.	325–374	VI–ii$\frac{6}{5}$–V7-I-V-I
CODA	375–426	i–VI–ii6–V7
	427–461	i–V7–i

V_7 at bar 181 (the retransition), which is prolonged through bar 212. Rather than proceed directly to the tonic and restatement of the opening theme, Mendelssohn inserts a new idea, a contrasting lyric idea, stated first on D^b (VI), then a step higher on E^b, which will return eventually to the dominant. Mendelssohn's reason for adding this section could be purely practical, that is, to separate the development section, which is based entirely on theme 1, and the statement of theme 1 at the beginning of the recapitulation. Or it could be related to our underlying narrative, a recollection of Fanny. In some respects this idea is reminiscent of the closing idea following the second theme in the first movement.

The recapitulation is relatively brief with a single statement of theme 1 and an extension leading to theme 2, which is divided into two parts, the first progressing to a cadence on the tonic and a second to a statement of theme 1 on D^b (VI). Some may take this to be the beginning of the coda, but, as we shall see, this extended passage plays an integral role in bringing the movement to a point of structural closure, though not necessarily to a point of psychological completion. The second theme had ended gently on V_7, and the function of this following statement seems to be, at least in part, to regain the energy necessary to arrive strongly at the tonic harmony in bar 375. This seems a more likely place to identify as the beginning of the coda. Meanwhile, note the approach to the cadence beginning in bar 362, the arpeggiation G_5–B^b_5–D^b_6 over the bass note $E^\natural$, reminiscent of the transition to the recapitulation in the first movement, but here leading instead to a triumphant ending.

The coda is divided into two sections, two grand statements of the first theme, the first beginning at bar 375, and the second, following a parenthetical digression (bars 391–421), at bar 427.

A foreground graph of the exposition, which omits certain passages not crucial to an understanding of the voice leading as it unfolds, is given in Example 1-10. The first theme is shown to reach the primary tone C_5 via arpeggiation over a tonic pedal, after which the phrase leads to a cadence on the dominant. Implied is the prolongation of C_5 by D_5, though the return to C_5 is displaced by a covering G_5. Not shown here is the extension of the dominant. In the repetition of the theme C_5 progresses up to E^b_5, which leads to D^b_5, the important upper neighbor, harmonized by the D^b chord in bar 29. As shown on the graph, this chord can be understood as the pivot in the modulation to the key of A^b (III). Not shown in the graph are the following seven bars, which have been inserted into the passage, delaying entrance of the diminished seventh chord in the new key. Though D^b appears to resolve momentarily to C_5 over an A^b chord in bar 42, this motion is internal to a passage leading to D^b_5, now harmonized as the seventh of the local dominant. This prepares the second theme, which is rather difficult to graph because of the imitative treatment of the four-bar idea moving from one voice to another, which explains the change in notation style.[13] This theme begins from an F minor chord (vi) and it leads eventually to D^b_5, supported by ii–V, before resolving to C_5/A^b. Not shown is the varied repetition

---

13 The voice leading has been indicated in two ways, with musical notation and below as intervals above the bass notes.

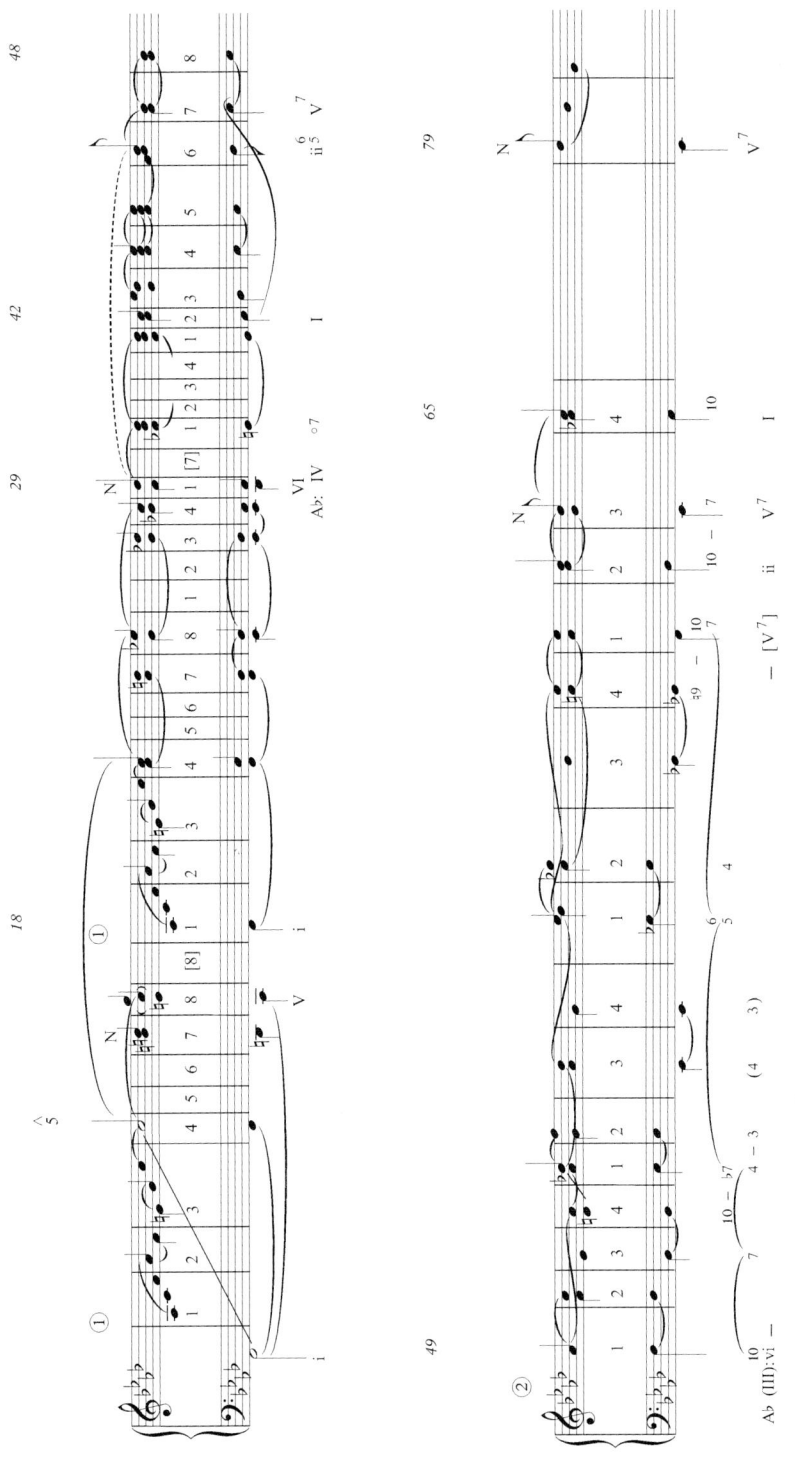

Example 1-10. Mendelssohn (IV): Foreground graph of the exposition

of this material, which is even more challenging to represent in graphic form due to the numerous registral changes as ideas move from one instrument to another. What is important for our discussion here is that the passage ends abruptly with D♭5 harmonized as the seventh of the dominant in bar 79, equivalent to the abrupt end of the exposition in the first movement.

A middleground interpretation of the voice leading of the development section and retransition is provided in Example 1-11. Before discussing this graph let's consider one issue related to hypermetric organization: successive downbeat measures. If you go back to the beginning of this movement, you will note that the first hypermetric unit, which starts in bar 2, is preceded by an upbeat measure, almost exactly as we observed in the first movement. The implication is that both movements begin with successive downbeat measures, and you might recall that this implication becomes explicit later in the development section of the first movement, at bars 112–113 and 141–142 (see Example 1-3). A similar situation occurs in the fourth movement: successive downbeat measures are found at the very beginning of the development (bars 81–82) and, looking ahead, at the beginning of the recapitulation (bars 269–270) and later in bars 325–326. It is a characteristic of the first theme.

Returning to Example 1-11, the division into parts is clearly notated both by vertical dotted lines and upper-case roman numerals above the top staff. The main features of Part I are the statement of the theme in F♭ major and the concurrent modal change of the primary tone to C♭. The extension of the theme returns via D♭5 to C♭5, now the third of an A♭ minor chord (bar 95), and later this process is repeated with D♭5, harmonized as the seventh of the dominant in A♭ resolving to C♮/A♭. The subsequent arpeggiation of the inner voice to A♭5 prepares Part II, which opens *ff* with an F7 chord leading eight bars later to the subdominant, first in the lower octave, but later an octave higher. Initially this idea is treated sequentially a step higher, but at bar 149, at the resolution of the G7 chord, Mendelssohn suddenly changes the pattern, which initiates a transition via v6 and i6 to Part III, which begins on iv6. Example 1-11 indicates that the connection between these two parts is the prolongation of the subdominant harmony by means of a voice exchange (bass and inner part), though this is not immediately apparent. Internal to this voice exchange are various registral changes, not all of which have been indicated to avoid too many crossing lines. For example, the seventh of the G7 chord is resolved to the bass of the v6 chord (indicated by the arrow), which leads to the inner voice F4 as part of the i6 chord (not shown), which is then transferred to F5 (top voice) at the beginning of Part III.

Part III of the development, which is relatively short, makes the connection between iv6 (D♭ bass) and V (C bass) via V of V. Melodically F5 leads to the inner voice E♮, which is covered by a motion from B♮5 leading up to C6, a realization of the resolution promised but aborted in the preceding part. Mendelssohn then sits on the dominant for thirty-one bars, first with C6 in the top part, then at the very end, on G5. This pitch has been marked ($\hat{2}$) on the graph to indicate its potential function (more on this below). Rather than proceed directly to the recapitulation, Mendelssohn inserts a lengthy digression, indicated in parentheses in Example 11.

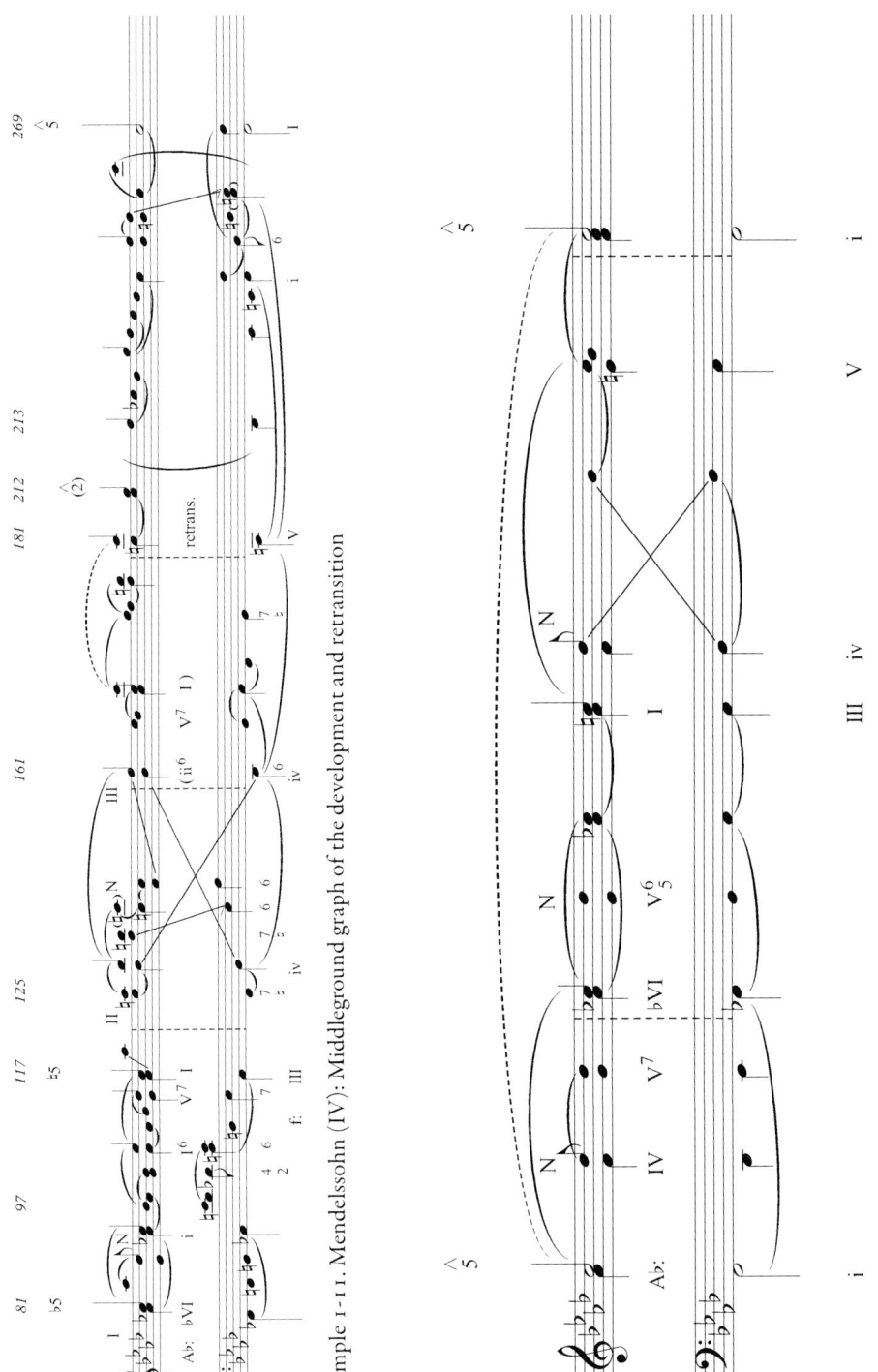

Example 1-11. Mendelssohn (IV): Middleground graph of the development and retransition

Example 1-12. Mendelssohn (IV): Deep middleground graph of the movement to the recapitulation

Our expectation from a Schenkerian perspective is that the fundamental line will lead to an interruption – that is, the fundamental line will descend to $\hat{2}$ /V – at the retransition, a prototype for sonata form movements in the minor mode. You might recall that in the first movement the fundamental line descends from $\hat{5}$ to $\hat{3}$ in the exposition, and we can posit a continuation to $\hat{2}$ supported by the diminished seventh chord at the retransition, though this $\hat{2}$ is weakly represented. In this fourth movement there is a very clear $\hat{2}$ /V (bar 212), which explains the notation in Example 1-11. So here we have a clear articulation of $\hat{2}$ /V, but there is no earlier descent from $\hat{5}$ to $\hat{3}$. There is no interruption, but rather $\hat{5}$ has been prolonged through the beginning of the recapitulation, where we can expect a structural descent to closure.[14] This view of the structure is given in Example 1-12, which shows the prolongation of C5 by its upper neighbor D$\flat$ at various levels of the structure.

A detailed graph of the recapitulation, including the extended passage beginning at bar 325, is offered as Example 1-13. The first theme re-establishes F minor and the primary tone C5, and, like the opening statement of the movement, it progresses from I to V. Not shown are the following extension of the dominant and transition to the second theme, which begins on D$\flat$ (VI). This graph attempts to represent the imitative entrances of the "subject" as clearly as possible, a task that requires some notational ingenuity. Most important is the descending third D$\flat$5–C5–B$\flat$4, indicated above the system as well as by the double curved slur. This descending third prepares the B$\flat$4 as seventh of the dominant, which resolves by implication to A$\flat$4 over tonic harmony at the conclusion of the initial statement of this material (bar 305). However, at the end of the varied repetition this B$\flat$4 resolves to A$\flat$4 over a D$\flat$ harmony at the beginning of the next section. The large slur above indicates the overall descent of a third C5–B$\flat$4–A$\flat$4 harmonized by the progression I–V7–VI.

A characteristic of the following extended passage is the shift to the upper octave, where the music remains almost exclusively for the remainder of the movement. The large slur from bar 326 to 348 indicates the statement of an answering third with a registral shift: A$\flat$4–G5–F5, where the goal is harmonized by a tonic chord in first inversion. Internal to this third is a prolongation of D$\flat$ (VI) with the top part arpeggiating to F6 before descending to F5, partially by step and partially by arpeggiation. The continuation beyond bar 348 is interesting in that Mendelssohn has chosen to return temporarily to the realm of D$\flat$ for eight bars, almost as if he were reluctant to relinquish a cherished memory. However, what follows is a definitive return to the tonic and a clear harmonization of the structural descent to closure. Again, we find scale degree 2 in the structural descent supported by the diminished seventh chord as substitute for the dominant. This allows the arpeggiation to continue to D$\flat$6 to introduce C6 once again over the implied arrival at $\hat{1}$. We may read closure at this point, but it is clear Mendelssohn has more to say.

---

14 A similar type of structure is discussed by Ernst Oster in a footnote (p. 139) to his translation of *Free Composition*.

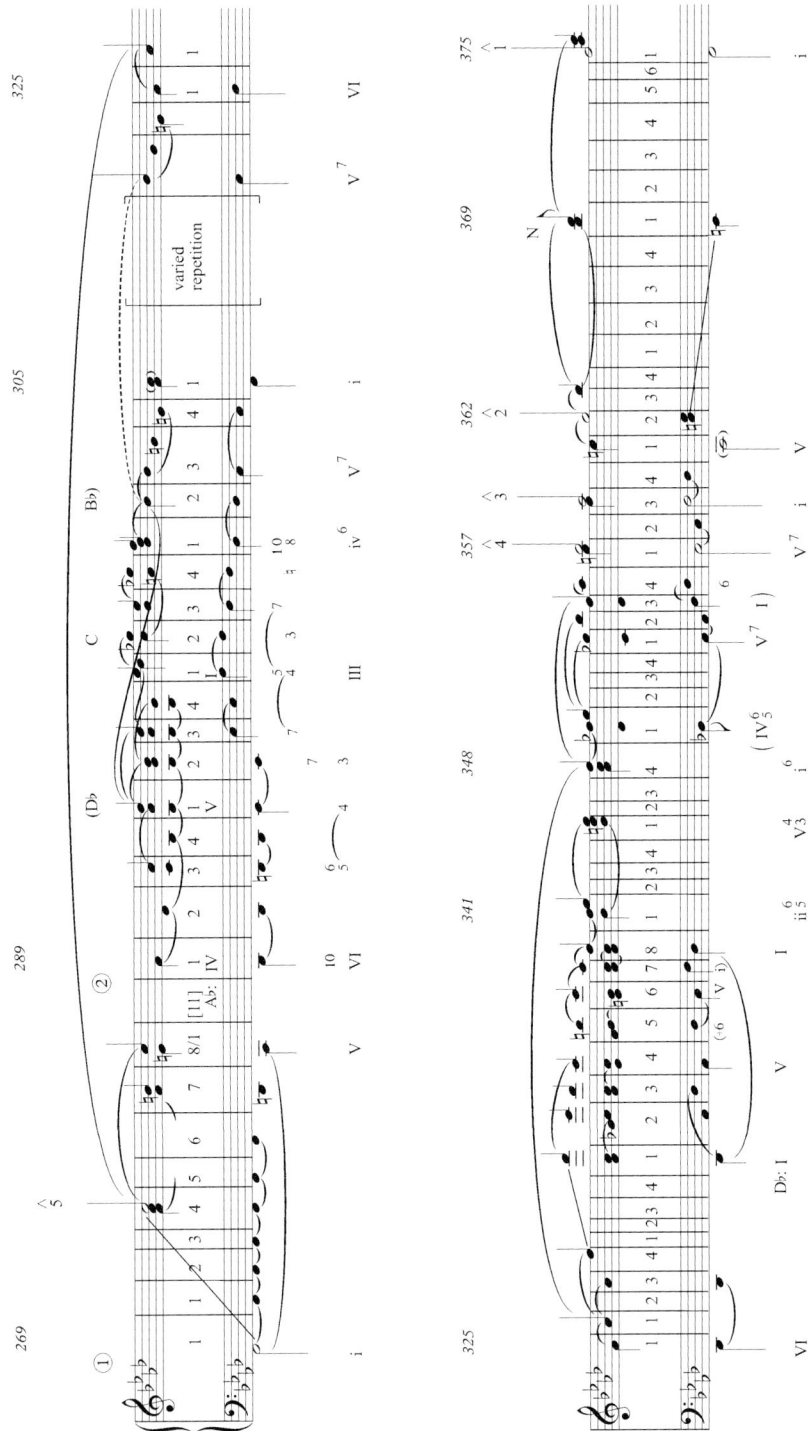

Example 1-13. Mendelssohn (IV): Foreground graph of the recapitulation

Example 1-14 presents an abstract overview of the recapitulation, where events are all represented in the lower octave. This graph indicates that the two extended descending thirds C–B♭–A♭ (bars 269–325) and A♭–G–F (bars 325–348) together form a descending fifth prolonging the tonic, and it reveals that the function of the prolonged D♭ can be understood as part of a descending arpeggiation in the bass connecting the tonic to the supertonic harmony in six-five position. All this is embedded within the structural descent of the fundamental line.

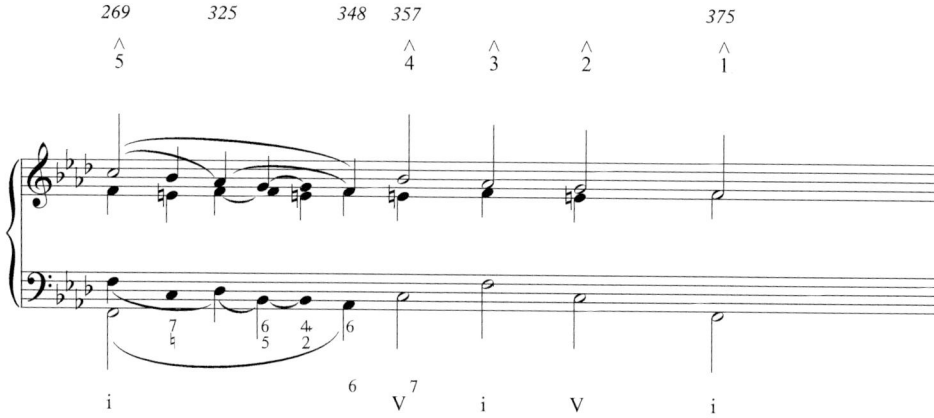

Example 1-14. Mendelssohn (IV): Deep structure of the recapitulation

The coda – the grand finale – is divided into two sections, bars 375–426 and 427–461. Both are initiated with statements of theme 1 by violin 2 covered by a running obligato (violin 1) originating from C6; both are stated emphatically (*ff*); and both contain descents of a fifth imitating and confirming the earlier structural descent. This is a strong ending to this movement, almost as if Mendelssohn's grief had been transformed to anger.

Chapter II

Schumann, piano quintet, op. 44, in e-flat major

The Piano Quintet was written in September-October of 1842, a year in which Schumann turned his attention to the writing of chamber music, including the three string quartets, op. 41, the piano quintet, op. 44, and the piano quartet, op. 47. Felix Mendelssohn played the piano part for the first private performance, substituting at the last minute for Clara, and he subsequently suggested some revisions, including the addition of a second trio to the scherzo movement. Most likely it would have been a revised version that Clara performed at the first public performance the following January and many times afterward.

In *Crossing Paths: Schubert, Schumann, and Brahms*, John Daverio chronicles Schumann's acquaintance with several of Schubert's works, including the second piano trio (D 929), which was singled out by Schumann for particularly high praise. There are, of course, striking similarities between the trio and Schumann's quintet. Both were written in the key of E-flat, both have funeral marches (in C minor) for their second movements, and both utilize ♭III (♭VI of the dominant) similarly for parenthetical digressions in the first theme areas of their first movements. Otherwise, they are very different works. Certainly, there is nothing in the Schubert, or for that matter in the first three movements of the Schumann, to predict the finale of the quintet, which, on the one hand, strikes out in an entirely new direction, while at the same time paying tribute to the past.

The year 1842 was for Schumann a time of intense interest in and study of the music of Bach, clearly reflected in this work by the two fugues at the triumphant ending. The subject of the final fugue is taken from the opening theme of the first movement with its distinctive ascending leap of a minor seventh, and Susan Wollenberg has suggested this idea may have its origin in the E-flat prelude from book I of the *Well-Tempered Clavier*.[1] Bach's influence is manifest in more subtle ways as well. A common feature of many of Bach's works in minor keys is a motion in the final phrase to the subdominant, allowing the work to end on a major tonic chord. Schumann adopts this practice in his second movement, though in this instance the motion to the subdominant is greatly expanded to include the final two sections of a seven-section movement. This is an enlargement of the emphasis on iv within the main theme of the movement.

The following analysis of the Schumann quintet will begin with an initial discussion of the formal design followed by a consideration of the voice leading at various levels. In addition, we must on occasion consider Schumann's interest in representing different personalities, e.g., Florestan and Eusebius, or their characteristics in his music, a speculative enterprise from an analytical perspective.

---

1 Susan Wollenberg, "Schumann's Piano Quintet in E-flat: the Bach Legacy," Ex. 1.

I. Allegro brillante

Overall, the design of the first movement is classical; that is, the outer shell, but not the content, could have been written fifty years earlier. The exposition, which is repeated, consists of two themes, the first in the tonic key and the second in the dominant. Following a transition, the development is divided into two parts, the first initiated from A♭ Minor (iv) and the second from F Minor (ii) leading to a retransition (V7). The recapitulation then follows the same path as the exposition, the main change being in the transition to the second theme, now in the tonic key rather than the dominant. In short, a classical design, but the content is pure Schumann, beginning with the boisterous first theme (representing Florestan), while the second theme is more lyrical (Eusebius).

A chart of the formal design is given in Table 2-1. The first theme area consists of two parts. The first, which is comprised of three overlapping phrases, leads from I to V. The second, which begins in G♭ Major (♭III), leads eventually to V of V via an augmented sixth chord in preparation for the second theme. Internal to the prolongation of G♭, which later functions as ♭VI in the key of the dominant, there is a brief modulation to E♭ Minor, not a real return to the tonic, but rather a reference to it within the extension of G♭. Table 2-1 shows theme 2 is also divided into two parts, though in this instance we are talking about two contrasting parts. The first (a) is a static idea, the opposite of the dynamic initial idea; it extends a single harmony (V in the new key), above which G displaces F, and this is followed by a beautiful duet between cello and viola (b). The entire theme is then restated with violin 1 joining the cello and viola in the b part of the theme. A third statement is initiated, but it is soon interrupted by a return to the character of the first theme and its emphasis on G♭ leading through an augmented sixth chord to V in preparation for the closing phrase, a modified statement of the main theme in the key of the dominant.

Both parts of the development are introduced by partial statements of the main theme, the first in the minor subdominant key beginning in bar 128 and the second in the supertonic in bar 167, the result being a middleground harmonic progression iv–ii–V7 (retransition), internal to which Schumann passes briefly through several other keys (all minor). In the recapitulation the first part of theme 1 is a repetition of its counterpart in the exposition. Part 2 then begins as before on G♭, which becomes the dominant of C♭, ♭VI in E♭, and the following motion to A♭ Minor is to be understood as internal to a prolongation of C♭, just as E♭ Minor was interpreted as an extension of G♭ at the equivalent place in the exposition. C♭ is then transformed into an augmented sixth chord leading to the dominant. The following statements of theme 2 replicate their statements in the exposition, now a fifth lower, and the following closing phrase, based on the initial theme, is expanded briefly to function as a coda.

A foreground representation of the first theme area – both parts 1 and 2 – is given in Example 2-1. The initial phrase (the theme) is shown to establish the primary tone G5 ($\hat{3}$) in bar 3, introduced by its upper neighbor, following the initial leap of a minor

TABLE 2-1. SCHUMANN (I): CHART OF THE FORMAL-TONAL DESIGN

EXPOSITION

First theme area				
Part 1			1–26	$E^\flat$: I–V
Part 2			27–50	$^\flat$ III/
				$B^\flat$:$^\flat$ VI–+6–V
Second theme area				
Statement 1		a	51–56	$B^\flat$: V^{7-6}
		b	57–72	I^{5-6} … V of V
Statement 2		a	73–78	
		b	79–94	
Statement 3		a interrupted	95–108	V^{7-6} [$^\flat$ VI–+6] V–I
Closing Phrase (th. 1)/codetta			108–117	I

DEVELOPMENT

transition		116–128	$B^\flat \to a^\flat$
Part 1		128–167	$a^\flat$ (iv)–$e^\flat$–$b^\flat$–C^7
Part 2		167–187	f(ii): $g^\flat$–$d^\flat$–$a^\flat$
retransition		187–206	$E^\flat$: V^7

RECAPITULATION

First theme area				
Part 1			207–232	$E^\flat$: I–V
Part 2			233–256	$^\flat$ III–$^\flat$ VI +6–V
Second theme area				
Statement 1		a	257–262	V^{7-6}
		b	263–279	I^{5-6} … V of V
Statement 2		a	280–284	
		b	285–300	
Statement 3		a ext.	301–314	V^{7-6} [$^\flat$ VI–+6] V–I
Coda (theme 1)			314–338	I

seventh $E^\flat4$–$D^\flat5$, the characteristic feature of this idea.[2] Overall, this theme descends a third $G5$–$F5$–$E^\flat5$.[3] The voice leading of the continuation involves the process of reaching over resulting in an ascending progression in parallel tenths between top voice and the bass

---

2 The purpose of the initial $E^\flat5$ in parentheses in the example is to show the origin of the ascending seventh as a descending motion by step. This notation will be used wherever this idea occurs.

3 Internal to this motion is a voice exchange between the outer voices (bars 1–7) which prolongs $G5/I$, which is not shown in Example 2-1 due to the amount of detail in the graph.

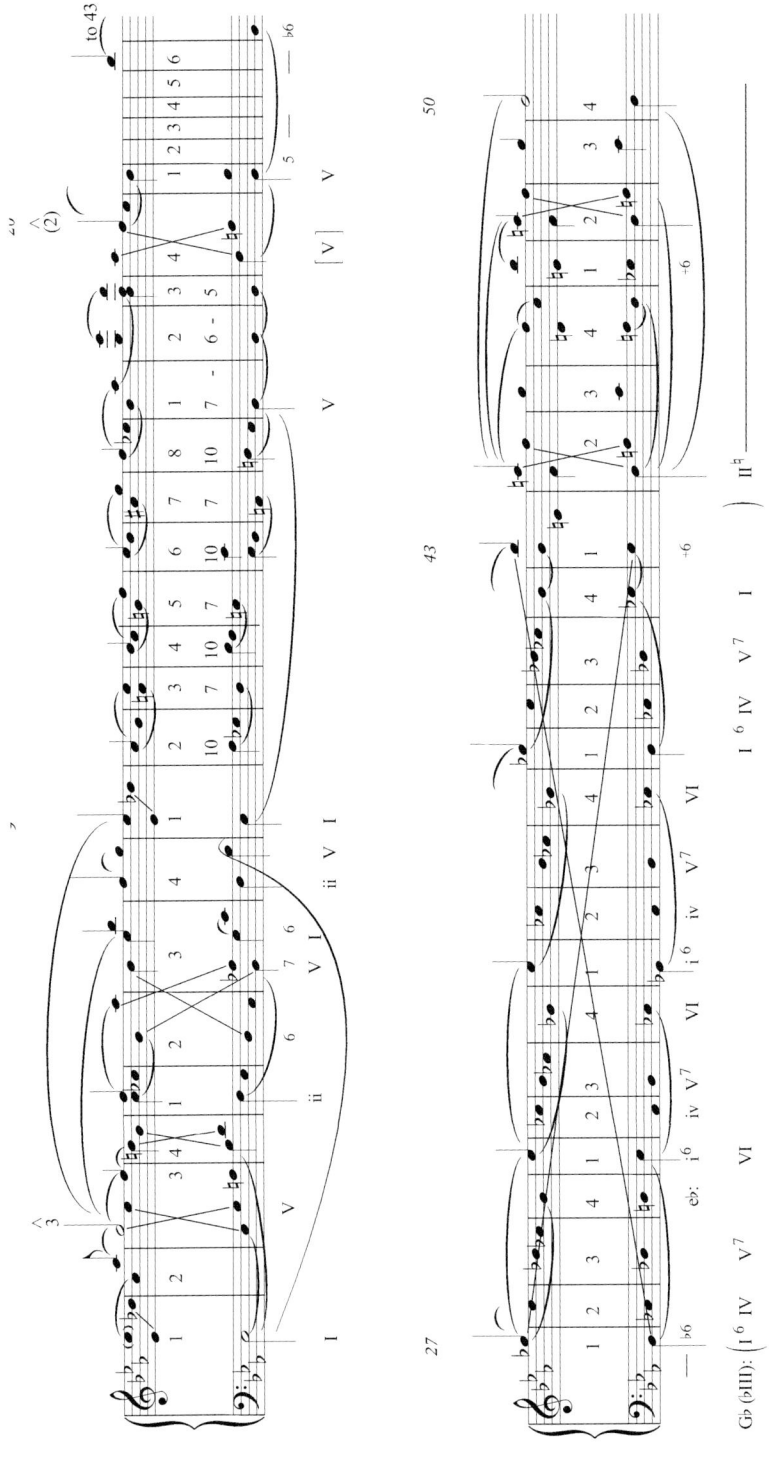

Example 2-1. Schumann (I): Foreground graph of the first theme area (exposition)

leading the top part from D5 to F5 supported by the dominant (bars 16–19), then confirmed by the following cadence. Melodically G5 has progressed to F5 (bar 20) supported by a motion from I to V over the span of this first part. The F5 in bar 20 has been marked $\hat{2}$ in parentheses to indicate a middleground representation of the interruption. In essence, if not in detail, this interpretation agrees with that given by Peter Smith in his article in *Rethinking Schumann*.[4] Part 2 then begins on a G♭ chord in first inversion (introduced by a 5-♭6 motion above the bass note B♭), and, though there is an excursion to E♭ Minor, this is shown as a motion internal to a prolongation of the G♭ harmony by a voice exchange (bars 27–43) transforming the G♭ chord into an augmented sixth chord leading to V of V, which is subsequently extended for eight bars.

Peter Smith identifies theme 2 as beginning in bar 57, the duet between cello and viola. In a certain sense he is correct; this is the idea we hear as the theme. But each time this idea appears it is preceded by a six-bar idea that I have characterized as static, since it is repetitive and consists of a single harmony, V in the new key. In its initial statement this creates an overlap between first and second theme areas, at the same time shifting the character of the dialogue. It is interesting to compare the voice leading of the b idea beginning in bar 57 to that of bars 10–17, the continuation of the first theme; though different in some respects, both progress in parallel tenths with the top part progressing from D5 back to F5, the controlling melodic note of both passages. In the third statement beginning in bar 95, the a idea is shortened from 6 to 4 bars, followed immediately by a four-bar parenthetical statement that recalls the G♭ harmony/augmented sixth of bars 27–43 delaying the descent of a fifth to local closure in bar 108. From a structural perspective the descent of a fifth from $\hat{2}$ within the second theme area is normative, though Schumann's realization of this idea is certainly unique.

Example 2-3 is arranged to show the correspondence between the two main parts of the development. The first progresses from iv to ii via an applied dominant (bars 130–169) supporting the descending third C♭6–B♭5–A♭5, and the second progresses ii–V7–I, first supporting A♭5 as a consonance and then as a dissonant seventh leading back to the primary tone G5. How all this fits into a larger context is shown in Example 2-4, a middleground graph of the structure of the exposition and development leading to the restatement. Part 1 of the first theme area is shown to be a lower-level interruption followed by the voice exchange transforming the G♭ chord into an augmented sixth chord leading to V of V at the cadence in bar 50. The F5 at this point is marked $\hat{2}$, the point of melodic interruption of the fundamental line, which is to be understood in relation to the following dominant, as indicated by the diagonal line. The exposition then ends with B♭5 as a covering tone preparing the continuation into the development. At the deepest level the development prolongs the dominant supporting the motion B♭5–A♭5 (8-7 of the dominant) leading to G5/I, a motion that is imitated in the foreground. At the middleground level the passing tone A♭5,

---

4 See "Associative Harmony, Tonal Pairing, and Middleground Structure in Schumann's Sonata Expositions," Ex. 12.1.

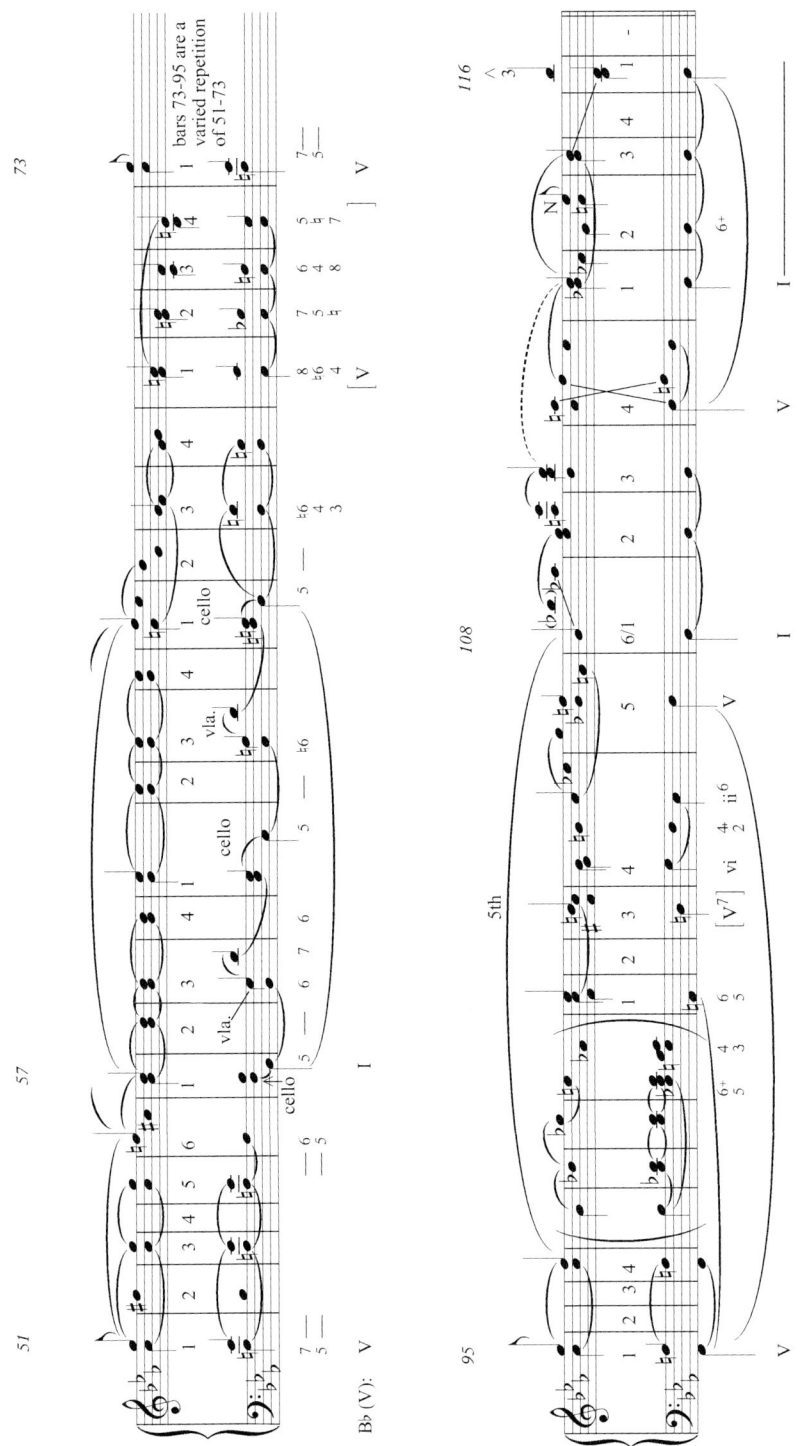

Example 2-2. Schumann (I): Foreground graph of the second theme area (exposition)

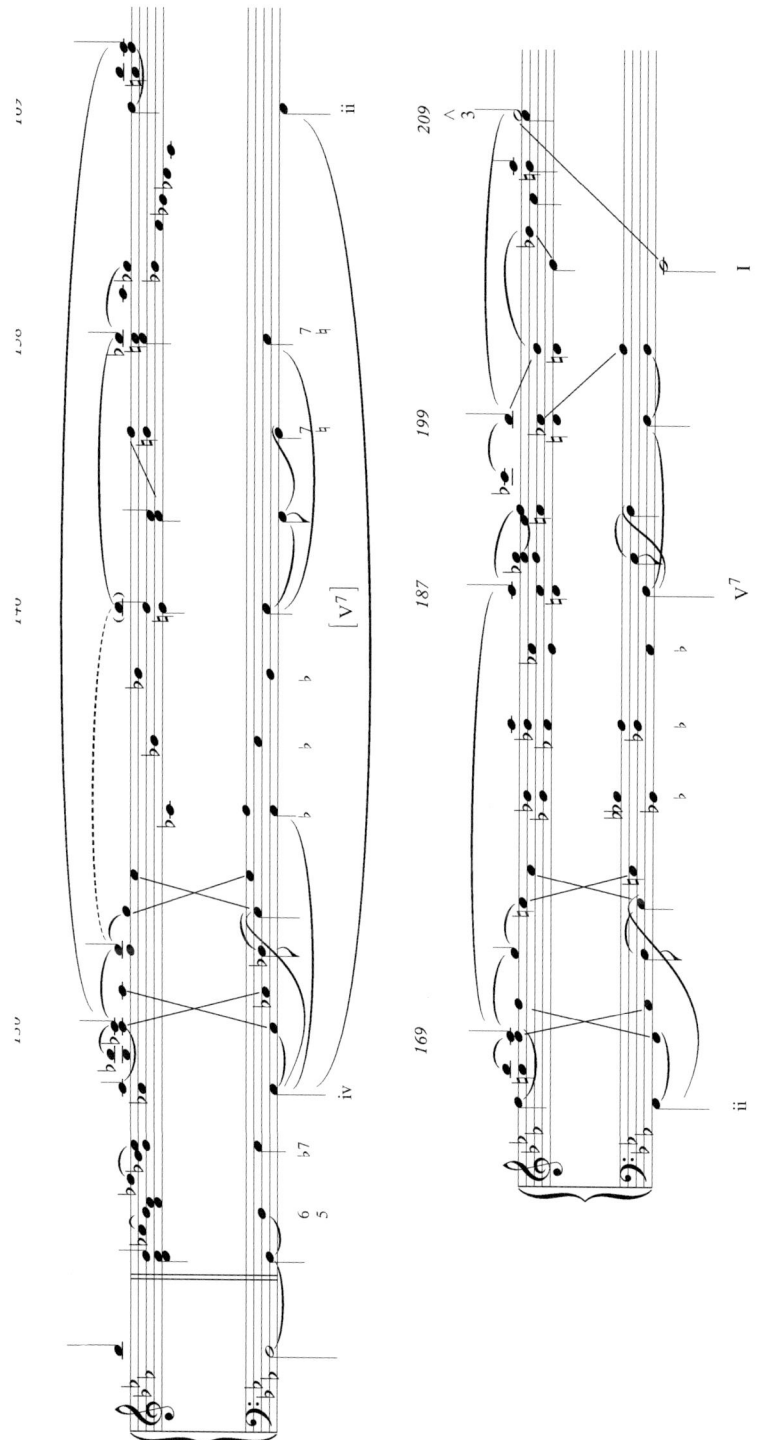

Example 2-3. Schumann (I): Middleground graph of the development

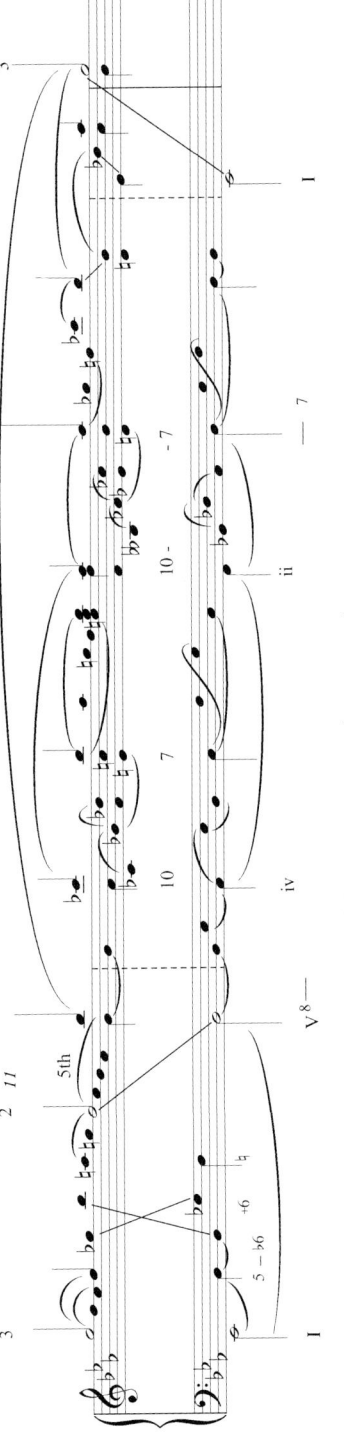

Example 2-4. Schumann (I): Middleground graph of the movement to the recapitulation

first supported by ii, then as seventh of the dominant, is approached by the descending third C♭6–B♭5–A♭5, a third progression embedded within the encompassing third B♭5–A♭5–G5.

Example 2-5 contains an accounting of the details of the harmony, voice leading and, beginning in bar 257, the hypermeter of the recapitulation following the repetition of bars 1–26. Part 1 of the first theme area ends with B♭5 covering F5, and in part 2 (bars 233–250) this covering line progresses through the passing tone C♭6, which is prolonged by the voice exchange transforming the C♭ chord into an augmented sixth, to D6/V.[5] Theme 2a, then, extends the dominant harmony, with C6 (the seventh above the bass) reintroducing the covering tone B♭5. The b phrase (the tune) begins on G5 and tonic harmony and progresses in parallel tenths with the bass back to B♭5, but, as suggested by the notation in the example, this G5 is not heard as an inner-voice tone, as was the D5 in the equivalent place in the exposition (bar 57), but now as the note being prolonged locally. In the third statement of this idea, the melodic line descends a fifth in conjunction with the completion of the fundamental line to closure,[6] which is even more forcefully stated in the coda (not shown) at bar 332.

---

5   In this example the voice exchange is shown to take place in bars 245–249 rather than bars 237–249 (which is correct) to avoid conflict with the detailed harmonic analysis between the staves.

6   It is very common in major key movements where the primary tone is $\hat{3}$ and the second theme is a descending fifth prolonging $\hat{2}$ in the exposition for closure of the fundamental line in the recapitulation to occur simultaneously with this fifth, now transposed to the tonic key.

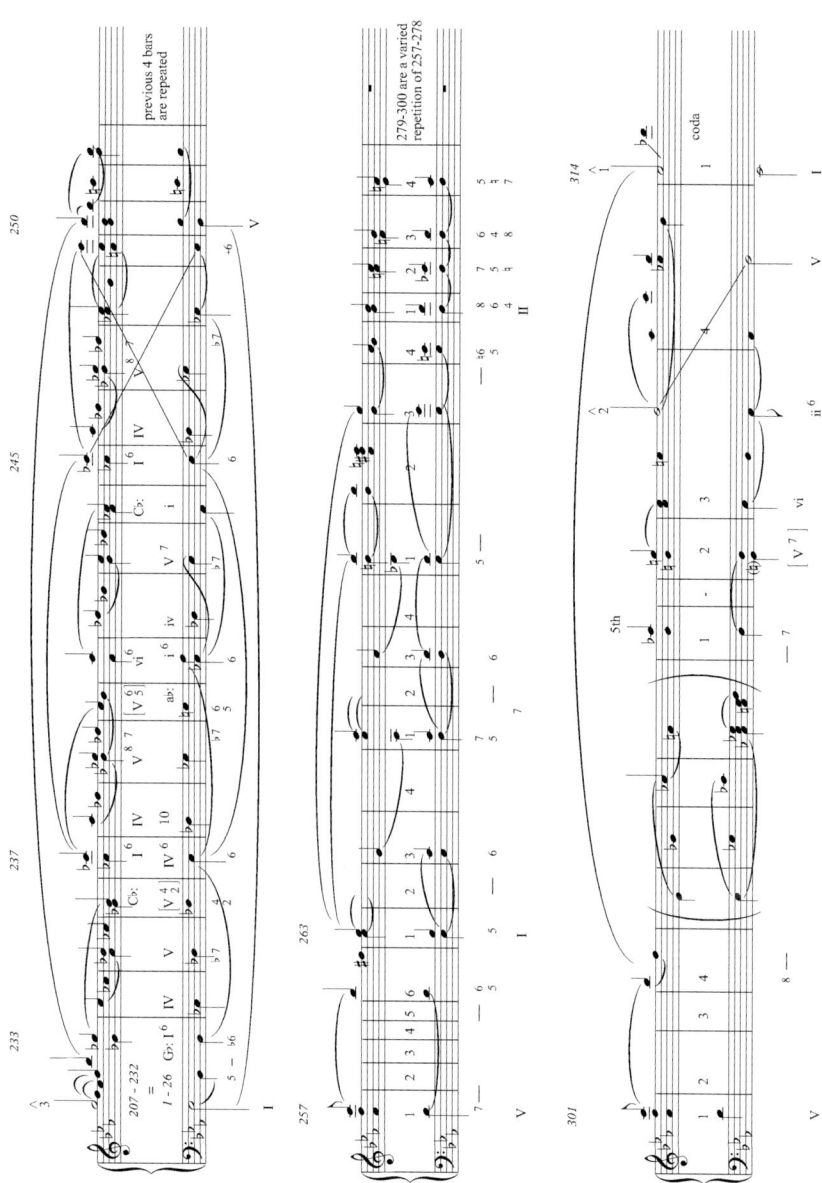

Example 2-5. Schumann (I): Foreground graph of the recapitulation

II. In modo d'una marcia, un poco largamente

This movement is a seven-part rondo: A¹–B¹–A²–C–A³–B²–A⁴, as outlined in Table 2-2. Each of the sections has some form of a ternary design, and the key scheme is c–C–c–f–c–F–f/c.

The main theme of the movement, bars 3–25, has the formal organization a (4+4) ||:b(4+4)–a'(4+4):||. The theme is introduced by a two-bar pickup (tonic harmony) and extended at the end by 4 bars reinforcing local closure in the tonic key (C Minor). A characteristic of the a idea is the emphasis given to the subdominant, a feature that is expanded

TABLE 2-2. SCHUMANN (II): CHART OF FORMAL-TONAL DESIGN

A¹			
	a	3–10	c: i
	||:b a' :||	11–25 (+4)	i–iv–V–i
B			
	c–c'	29b–45a'	C: I–V, I–V–I
	||: d–c'' :||	45–61a'	[V] iii, ii–V–I
A²			
	a	62–69	c: i
	b	70–77	i–iv
	a'	77–84	iv–V–i
trans		84–91	[o7] iv
C [agitato]			
	e	92–96, 96–100	f: i–V–i
	||: f–e :||	100–105, 105–109	i–V–i
A³			
	a	110–117	c: iv–V–i
	b	118–125	→ iv
	a'	125–132a	iv–V–i
B²			
	c–c'	132b–139, 139–148a'	F: I–V, I–V–I
	d	148b–156	[V] iii
	c''	156–164	ii–V–I
A⁴			
	a	165–172	f: iv–V–i⁶/
			c: iv⁶–V–i
	b	173–180	VII– iv
	a' ext.	180–193	iv–V–I

later in the movement, first in the C section (F Minor), then in B² (F Major) and in the final section as well, which begins in the subdominant key. A foreground graph of this first theme is provided in Example 2-6. The initial melodic gesture introduces G4, a covering tone of the primary tone E♭4 ($\hat{3}$) introduced first in bar 5. The initial melodic descent G4–F4–E♭4 is harmonized by a motion to VI uniting the two phrases, and the second descent, then, leads to local closure. The b section contains two phrases, the first consisting of a descending fourth E♭4–D4–C4–B♭3 harmonized by a motion to B♭ (VII) and, following a transfer to the upper octave, the second a descending fourth B♭4–A♭4–G4–F4 leading to a cadence on iv. At a deeper level this results in a step progression E♭4/i (bar 12) to F4/iv (bar 18), which is both a point of arrival and a point of departure (4/1), in short, a point of metric reinterpretation in the hypermeter. The result of this local modulation to iv and this metric overlap is to give further emphasis to the subdominant as the point of departure for the a′ phrase.

The A¹ section ends in the first half of bar 29, and the B¹ section begins immediately in the second half of the same bar. This second section is maximally different from the preceding one: first, it is written in the major tonic key; second, it has a new distinctive accompaniment (quarter-note triplets [piano] vs. eighth notes [inner strings]); and third, the initial melodic phrase, marked c in the chart and in Example 2-7, is static, hardly straying from the local primary tone, E5. The first two phrases exhibit a $\hat{3} - \hat{2} // \hat{3} - \hat{2} - \hat{1}$ structure, where $\hat{2}$ is initially approached by a descending third F5-E5-D5. The accompaniment persists in the d phrase, as does the character of the melodic writing, but here there is some relief from the stasis of the preceding phrase by means of the modulation to E Minor (iii) and the corresponding descent of the melodic line to the lower octave (E4). The return to the c″ phrase is accomplished via a 5–6 motion above the bass note E, saving the dominant for the descent to local closure in bar 61.

A foreground graph of the C and A³ sections is provided in Example 2-8. The main feature of the *agitato* C section is the prolongation of A♭4/A♭5, the upper neighbor of the covering tone from the A¹ section, and the subdominant harmony. Initially A♭4 is prolonged by its upper neighbor after which A♭5 is approached by an ascending third F5–G5–A♭5. This phrase is then repeated an octave higher. The following contrasting phrase (f) emphasizes the subdominant in the local key, which is prolonged by a voice exchange, as shown in Example 2-8. This leads to a repetition of the ascending third to regain A♭5. The following varied repetition of the opening phrase does not lead to local closure, but remains fixed on A♭5. The subsequent return to A material (A³) is different from before in two respects: first, the triplet accompaniment from the preceding section is continued (piano) and the melody is stated in an inner voice (initially by the viola, but in the final phrase by the piano), as highlighted in the example by the arrows.

Voice-leading graphs of the final two sections have not been provided, but instead an overview of the entire movement in relation to the formal divisions (Example 2-9). Note the extension of the subdominant from B² into A⁴. The abbreviated graph shows the motion to closure first within iv, then in the tonic. As noted in the introductory comments to

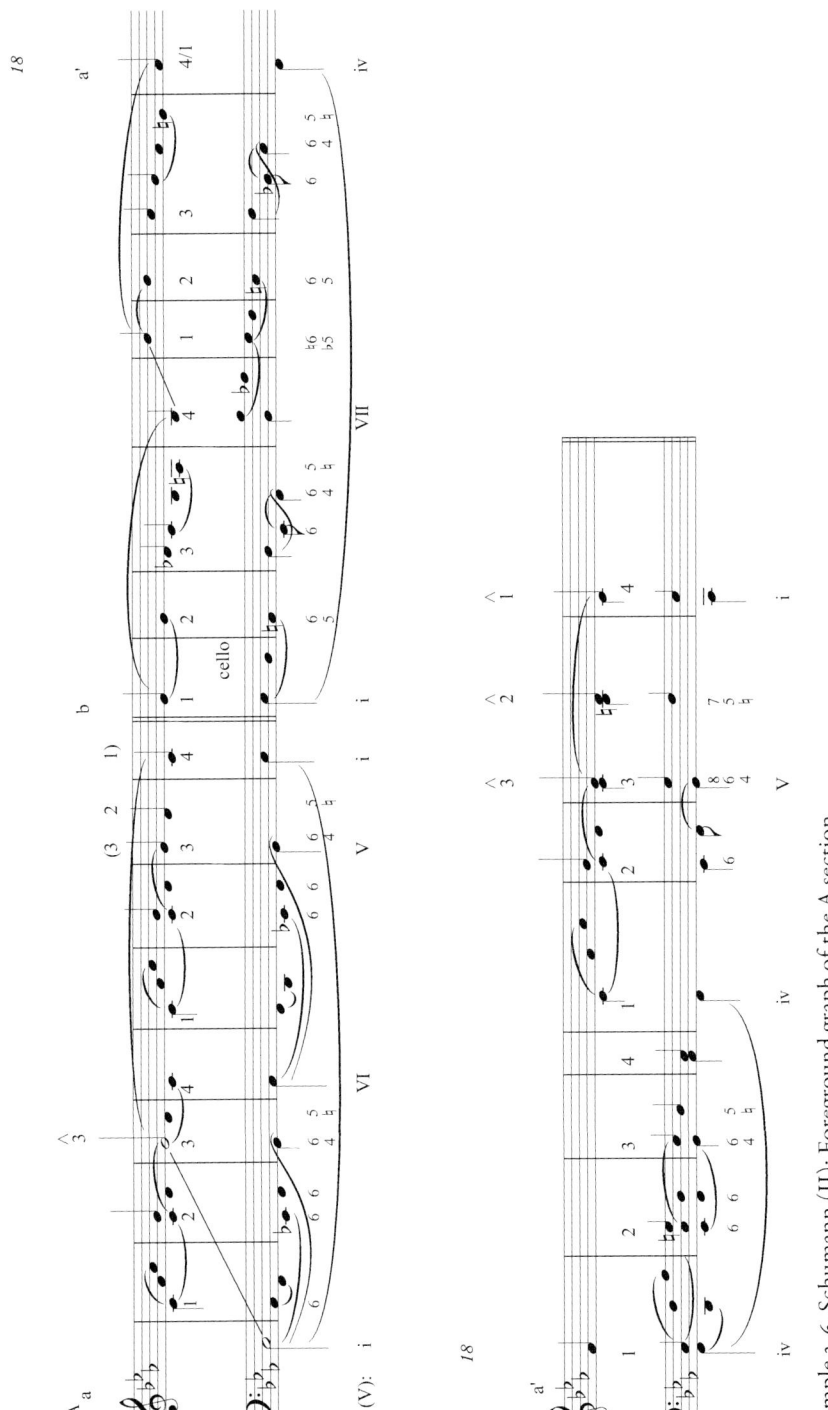

Example 2-6. Schumann (II): Foreground graph of the A section

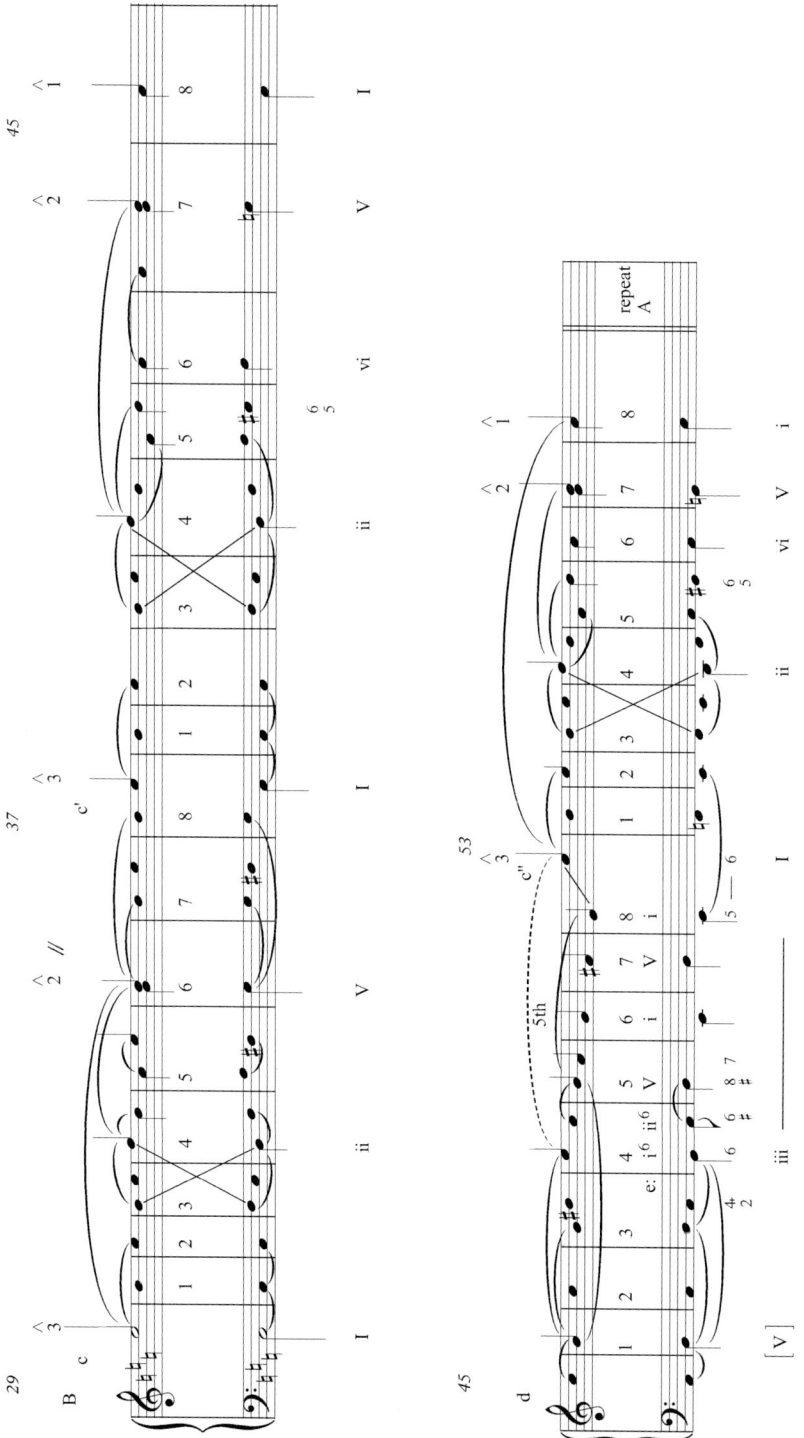

Example 2-7. Schumann (II): Foreground graph of the B section

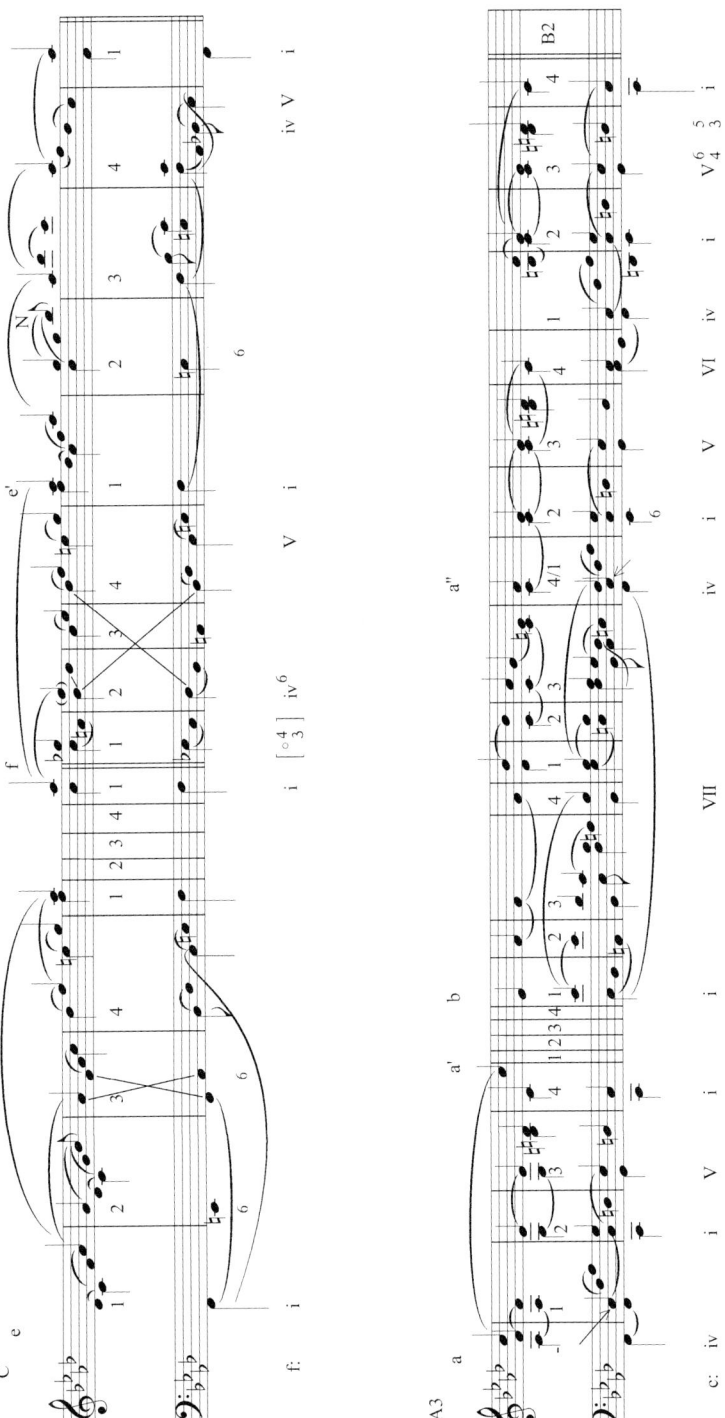

Example 2-8. Schumann (II): Foreground graph of the C and A3 sections

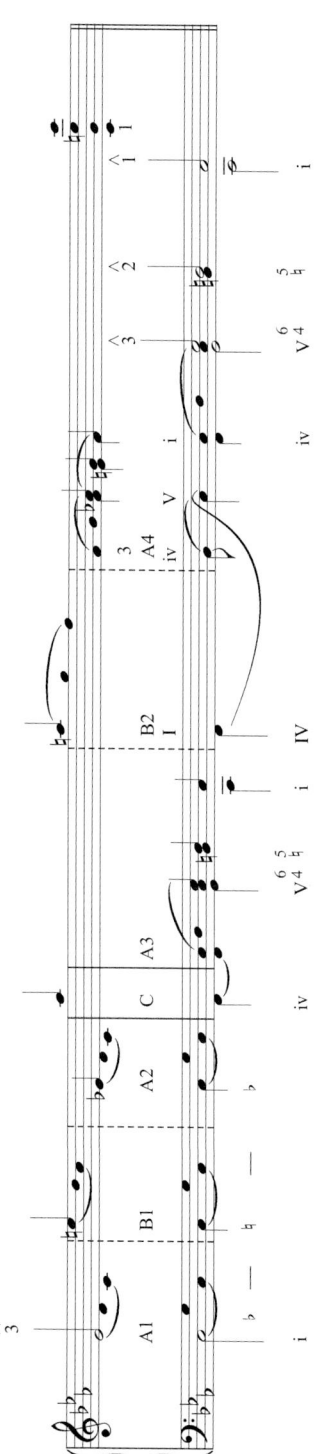

Example 2-9. Schumann (II): Overview of the entire movement

this chapter, the movement ends on a major chord, reminiscent of the way Bach had ended many of his works in minor keys. Schumann prepares this by the increasing emphasis on iv as the movement progresses, but locally by the approach to the final chord in bars 186–193.

III. Scherzo, molto vivace

Though the preceding march ends with a major chord (harmonics), this is a dark somber movement, particularly so with the closing statements of the main idea by the viola with the raw sound of the open c string. Suddenly with the scherzo we are thrust into a very different sound world, a bright energetic world of cascading scales, syncopations, and punctuated goals along the way. A graph of the scherzo showing only its essential structural features is offered in Example 2-10. Following the initial establishment of the primary tone G ($\hat{3}$) in bar 8, the first part (A) consists of two parallel motions, a descending fifth from D5 to G4 harmonized by iii and a descending fifth from F4 to B♭3 harmonized by V. As indicated by the bass slur, the harmony of this first part progresses I–iii–V, a motion that is embedded within the encompassing I–IV–V7–I across the A′ and B sections to A′. This progression supports the ascending fourth B♭4–C5–D5–E♭5, above which the primary tone is reintroduced by its upper neighbor A♭5, which has been approached from above. The A′ section repeats a condensed version of this same ascending fourth – a motivic parallelism – with D5 substituting for the implied F5 ($\hat{2}$) in the initial descent of the fundamental line.

In contrast to the scherzo, which conveys a sense of expansiveness, trio 1 involves imitative statements of a four-bar idea initially stated by violin 1. The first note of each statement is indicated in Example 2-11 by an arrow. The key of the trio is G♭ Major (♭III), the key of the second part of theme 1 from the first movement, though the harmony of the initial four-bar statement opens with the subdominant, the initial support for G♭5 ($\hat{3}$). The B section continues the imitative treatment with a variant of the original four-bar idea. This section is written in the key of B♭ Minor (iii in G♭), which supports F5, locally $\hat{2}$. Overall, the harmony of the trio after the establishment of G♭ is I–iii–IV–I–V7–I. The following retransition leads back to the tonic (E♭) via V7, resulting in the following harmonic plan for the original movement (with no trio 2):

I (scherzo)–♭III (trio 1)–V7 (retransition)–I (scherzo)

Example 2-12 is a middleground graph of the added second trio, which consists of numerous statements of two short harmonic progressions: i–iv–V–I and ♭II–V–i. What is initially confusing about this trio from an analytic perspective is Schumann's notation of keys, which in some cases were clearly chosen with the performer in mind rather than a notation reflecting their function. For example, C♭ Minor is mercifully notated as B Minor. Some of the keys have been re-notated in Example 1-12 to show their function and to make sense of the progression. Overall, trio 2 is in the key of A♭ Minor (iv), which supports

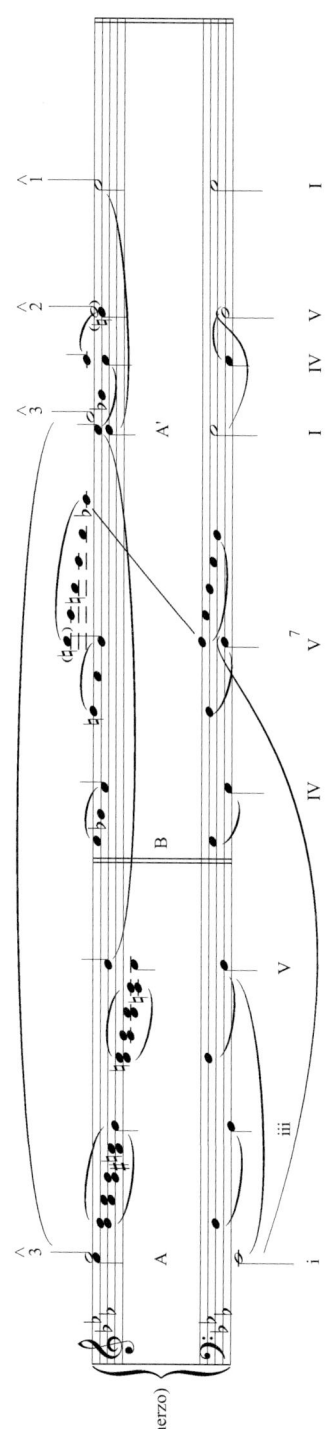

Example 2-10. Schumann (III): Middleground graph of the scherzo

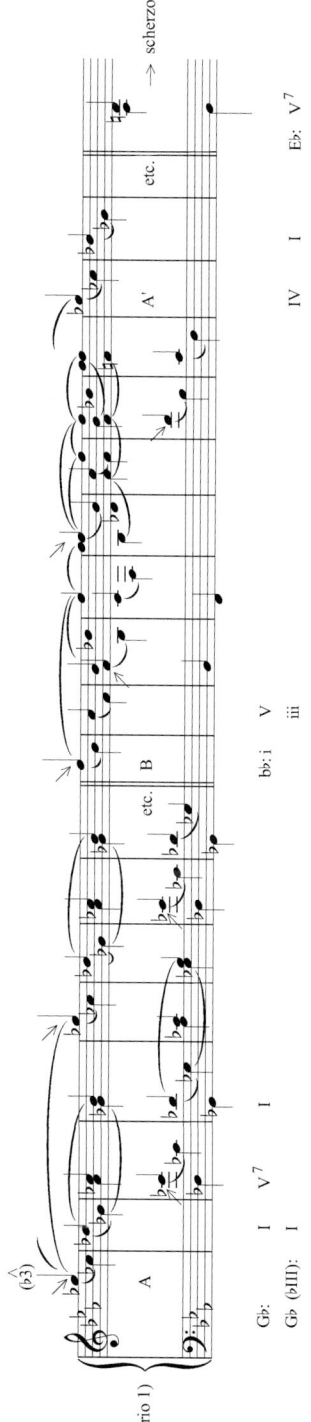

Example 2-11. Schumann (III): Foreground graph of trio I

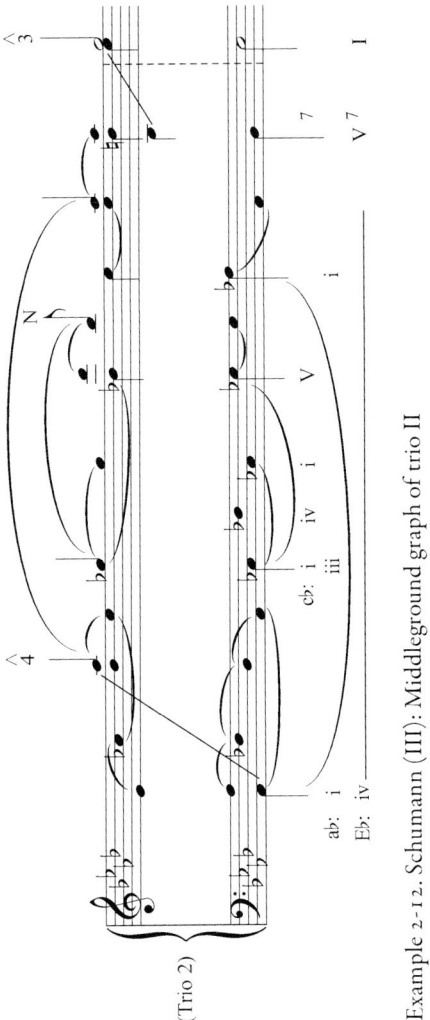

Example 2-12. Schumann (III): Middleground graph of trio II

A♭5, the upper neighbor of the primary tone, to which it resolves after being harmonized as the seventh of the dominant. Initially A♭ Minor is prolonged by a descending progression in thirds: a♭–E[F♭]–C♯[D♭]–a♭. The next series of keys (written as b–a–b–f♯) prolongs c♭ (iii); they support G♭5, which reaches up to B♭5 to re-state A♭5 in preparation for the return to the local tonic.

In the A section of the scherzo and in both trios the intermediary key is the mediant. In the finale, the movement begins in the mediant key, G Minor/G Major.

IV. Allegro ma non troppo

The first three movements of this quintet are relatively conventional in terms of their design and structure (though certainly unique in their content), but this fourth movement must be understood as a radical departure from the past. There are remnants of a formal convention here, even a clear nod to tradition, but this is a very unusual movement for the time, a product of a very inventive and fertile imagination. The first 212 bars resemble a sonata movement in terms of formal design, but from a tonal perspective this portion of the movement is decidedly atypical in that the tonic of E♭ is not established until the end of the "recapitulation". Table 2-3 divides this portion of the movement into three parts: I, Initial Statement of Ideas [exposition]; II, Digression [development]; and III, Restatement of Ideas [recapitulation]. The fourth part, labelled Extended Coda in the Table[7], opens with the initial melodic idea of the movement, and, following a transition passage, it leads to a fugato based on this idea. At this point we might expect a build-up to a climax and a triumphal ending to the movement. Instead, Schumann surprises us by adding a fugue on the main theme from the first movement with a countersubject based on the initial idea from this movement. This is a very effective way to tie the four movements together into a unified whole, but it also raises a potential question regarding the genesis of this last movement. It is possible the movement developed in time as it exists, that is, from beginning to end with a last-minute decision to add the fugue. But it is also possible the idea of the fugue came earlier. What has generated this speculation is the use of the main theme of the movement as the countersubject. If Schumann conceived of the fugue first, then it seems possible that the movement may have grown out of this material.[8]

In the preface it was noted that a complete understanding of Schumann's style sometimes requires dealing with his interest in representing different personalities in his music. So far this has been done only in passing in the first movement by characterizing the first theme as representing Florestan and the second theme Eusebius. This view of Schumann's writing becomes crucial in this movement, particularly in the "development" section. Table 2-3 identifies three ideas that represent three different persons/personalities, labelled simply as a, b, and c.[9] The prevailing tonality of the first part, initially established by the statements of a in bars 1–9 and again in bars 14–21 is G Minor (iii), which is changed to major toward the end of the exposition. Motive a is a bold idea in comparison to b, a scalar passage in E♭ (the *real* tonic). The reference to E♭ here is intriguing. Earlier, in the first and third movements, the mediant tonality is heard in relation to the tonic. Here the real

---

7 A somewhat different conception of the form of this movement is given by Julie Hedges Brown in her article "Schumann and the *style hongrois*". She divides the movement into two large parts, the first containing the exposition, development, and recapitulation, and the second containing a coda for the movement followed by a coda for the quintet.

8 The only way to test this speculation would be to have access to earlier drafts and sketches.

9 It is certainly possible these three represent Florestan, Eusebius, and Meister Raro, but these names will not be used here.

TABLE 2-3. SCHUMANN (IV): CHART OF FORMAL-TONAL DESIGN

PART I: INITIAL STATEMENT OF IDEAS

a,a	1–5, 5–9	G minor (iii)
( )	9–14	E♭: V–I–[V]–vi
a,a	14–18, 18–21	G minor
b,b	21–25, 25–29	E♭: I
a,a	29–33, 33–36	D minor
b	36–43	E♭: V
trans. (based on b)	43–51	G major
c (multiple statements)	51–69	G minor
b	69–77	G minor

PART II: DIGRESSION

a,a	77–81, 81–85	B minor
fanfare	85–93	B major
attempts by b to be heard	93–114	B7
c with counter melody	114–130	B7–D#7
c in octaves	130–136	B

PART III: RESTATEMENT OF IDEAS

a,a	136–140, 140–144	G# minor
( )	144–148	E: V–I–[V]–vi
a,a	148–152, 152–156	D# minor
b,b	156–160, 160–164	B = V of E
a,a	164–168, 168–172	B♭ minor
b	172–178	G♭–B♭
trans. (based on b)	178–186	E♭: I–vi–ii
c (multiple statements)	186–204	V–I–IV–V
b	204–212	♭VI–+6–V–I

PART IV: EXTENDED CODA

a extended	212–224	E♭: I–iii–V–I
trans. (based on c and a)	224–248	V–I
fugato (a)	248–274	I
c and extension to cadence	274–300	V–I
extension of cadence	300–318	I [+6/5 V] V7
fugue		
entrances	319–355	I
stretto	355–378	V–I
closing section		
transition	378–402	I
extension of tonic	402–427	I

tonic is heard locally in the context of the mediant, though those with reasonable tonal memory will certainly recognize E♭ as the real tonic. It seems Schumann is playing with this ambiguity. Until bar 51 our attention vacillates between a and b, but once c enters, it is stated several times.

The development opens with two statements of a in B minor. This is followed by what is best described as a fanfare in B Major imitating a brass band, as if to introduce someone or something important. What ensues may be described as various attempts by b to enter the conversation, only to be cut short by c or brief remnants of the fanfare. Then in the second half of bar 114 c enters, first in the viola part, then the cello, and finally violin 1 accompanied throughout by a new idea (an outgrowth from the fanfare) before being stated emphatically by all instruments together in bar 130. Personality b did manage to be heard after several unsuccessful attempts, but c takes over and dominates the conversation. The ensuing recapitulation follows with the same sequence of events as the exposition, however beginning a half step higher in G♯ minor (enharmonically iv) and D♯ Minor, and initial statements of b in E Major and its dominant. An important change occurs tonally with the statements of a in B♭ Minor and the following statements of b in G♭ (a reference to the first movement) and B♭, the dominant. Over the span of the recapitulation to this point the minor subdominant has made its way to the dominant. It is then through the following statements of b and c that E♭ is now firmly established as the tonic.

Part 4, like the preceding parts, opens with two statements of a, which are extended to introduce a lengthy transitional passage leading to the fugato on a. This transitional passage is based primarily on a syncopated version of c, where the original motion by step is replaced by leaps. There are also brief references to a (cello) beginning in bar 240 in anticipation of the fugato. This passage ends on the tonic (bar 248); however, the initial fugal entrance of a is stated at the same pitch level as it was in the beginning of the movement, resulting in a temporary recall of G Minor (iii). The fugato ends on a G major chord in bar 274, introduced as if it might lead to C Minor, but the following passage, based on statements of c, progresses instead to a climactic cadence on the tonic in bar 300. The extension of the cadence then proceeds to the dramatic introduction of the fugue. The harmony of this climactic passage (bars 312–318) is I^6 passing through an augmented sixth chord (spelled as a G♭ 7chord) to the dominant. The following fugue is divided into two parts, first a series of entrances ending on the dominant in bar 355, and second a stretto passage ending on the tonic in bar 378. The continuation, which leads to the triumphal ending, recalls the earlier transition beginning in bar 224.

Example 2-13 is organized to show the relationship between the voice leading of the first part and statements of a, b, and c, which are indicated between the staves. The statements of a and b in the first 41 bars are also separated on the graph by vertical dotted lines. As noted in the previous discussion of the design of this movement, the prevailing tonality of this first part is G Minor/Major with interjections by b (and later by the four-bar parenthetical statement delaying the cadence) recalling but also anticipating E♭ as the true tonic. The initial statement of a opens with an arpeggiation to G5, anticipating what

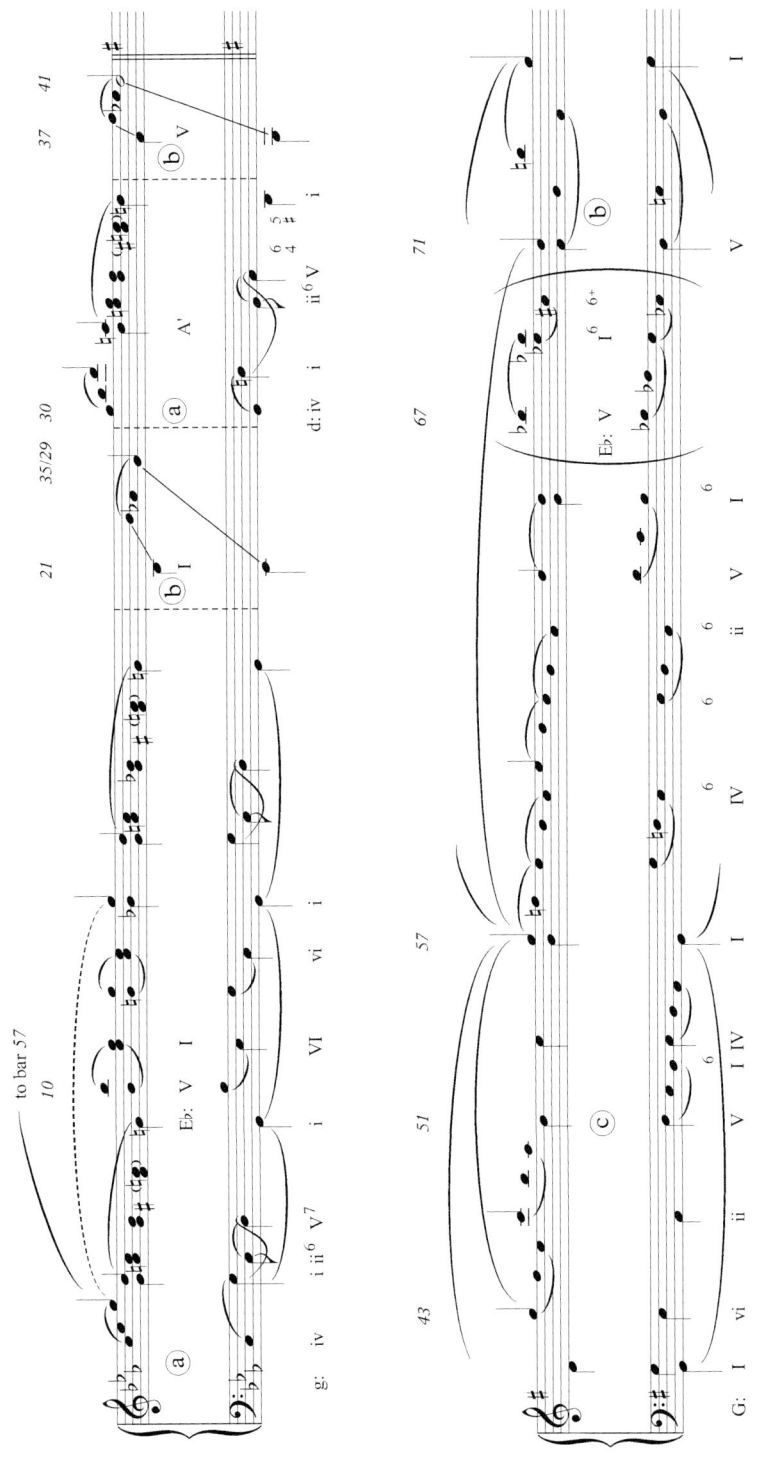

Example 2-13. Schumann (IV): Middleground graph of part I

will emerge in the fourth part as the primary tone. The arpeggiation figure, supported by subdominant harmony, is followed by a descending fifth with the leading tone substituting for the second scale degree; the notation used here, showing the implied second scale-degree in parentheses, will be employed throughout wherever a appears. After the initial statements of a and b, each is stated a fifth higher, closing out the section in G Minor. At a deeper level, Example 2-13 shows the prolongation of $G5$ throughout, first from the beginning to bar 57, then, following a descent to $D5$, to the end of the exposition.

As suggested by the earlier description of the development section, one way to understand this portion of the movement is to imagine a conversation involving the three personalities. As always, a opens the dialogue, and after a brass-like fanfare, b makes various attempts to be heard, only to be cut off. Then, when c finally enters, that personality gradually dominates the conversation. The overall tonality of this part of the movement is B Minor/Major, the mediant in G. As shown in Example 2-14, $F\sharp5$, the lower neighbor of $G5$, is prolonged throughout this section. This pitch is initially stated by a and prolonged locally by the descending fifth, restated in lower octaves in the fanfare and again by c and the covering remnants of the fanfare beginning in bar 101. The final statement of this descending fifth from $F\sharp5$ is generated from the melody covering c at bar 115. Following the interjection by a $D\sharp7$ chord, which anticipates the opening tonality of the recapitulation, the fifth is completed in the lower octave.

The recapitulation opens with statements of a in G♯ Minor, enharmonically A♭ Minor (iv), and its dominant, and the following statement of b is on the mediant B (=C♭). Once again, we encounter Schumann, the practical musician, notating for ease in reading. And though the following statement of a in B♭ Minor/Major appears to be a major shift from the sharp to the flat side, in reality the progression from bar 137 to 165–178 is from subdominant to dominant, as indicated below the staff in Example 2-15. The interjection by b in bar 172 is a fifth above the earlier statement on B/C♭. At the same time this would seem to be a reference to the employment of G♭ (♭III) in the first theme area of the first movement, yet another example of "associative harmony".[10] Following the extension of the dominant harmony, the music finally reaches the tonic briefly at bar 192, which, with the immediate addition of D♭,[11] becomes V of the subdominant. This subdominant is subsequently prolonged by a chromatic voice exchange transforming it into an augmented sixth chord before the cadence on E♭.

With the statement of a at the beginning of the Extended Coda the primary tone is firmly established, then, following the extended passage prolonging the dominant, stated again at the beginning of the fugato. Example 2-16 does not provide a detailed sketch of the fugato, rather indicating only the descending fifths of the entrances and the retention

---

10 See, for example, Peter Smith's article "Associative Harmony. Tonal Pairing, and Middleground Structures in Schumann's Expositions".

11 Though possibly a stretch, the addition of D♭ here could be taken as a passing reference to the opening theme of the quintet, not just a product of a standard cadential progression.

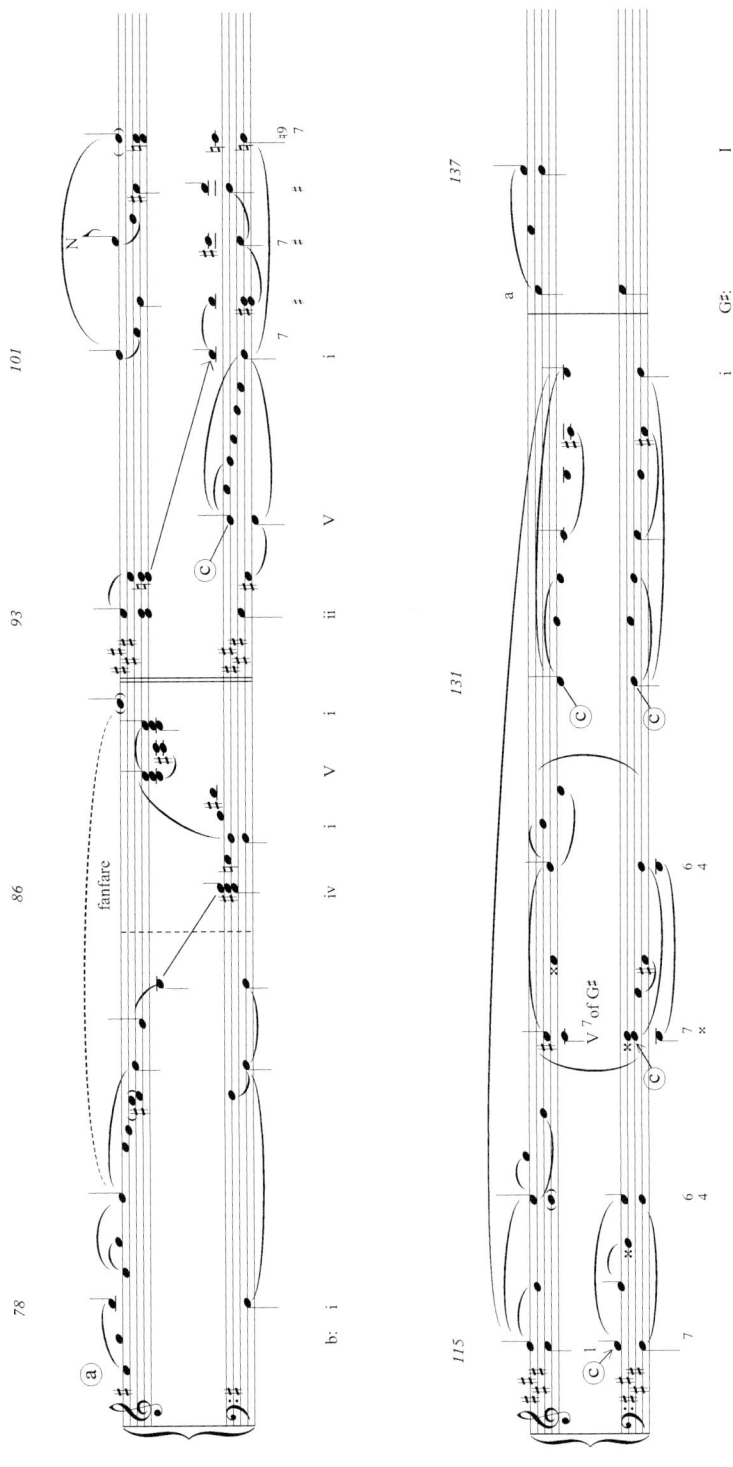

Example 2-14. Schumann (IV): Middleground graph of part II

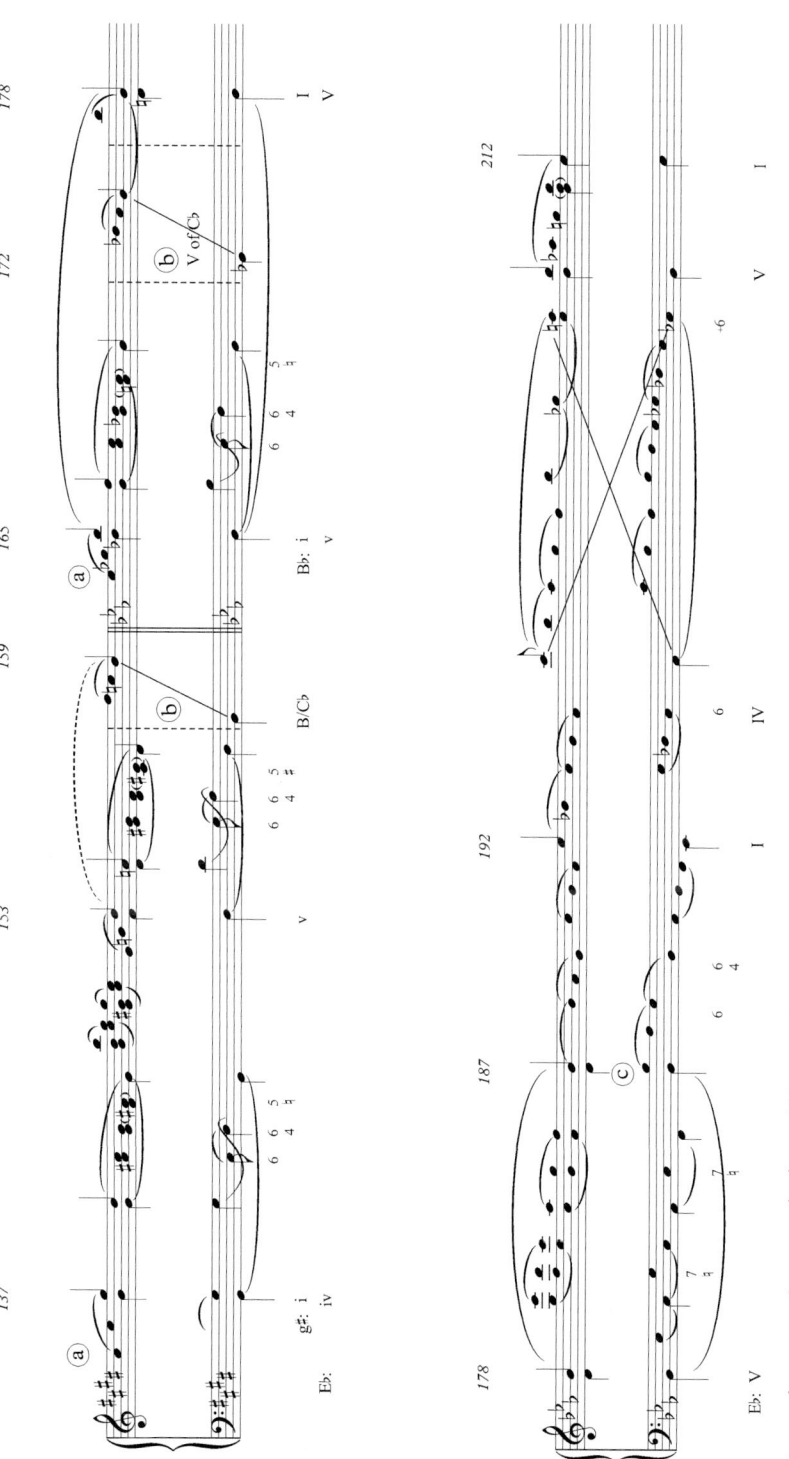

Example 2-15. Schumann (IV): Middleground graph of part III

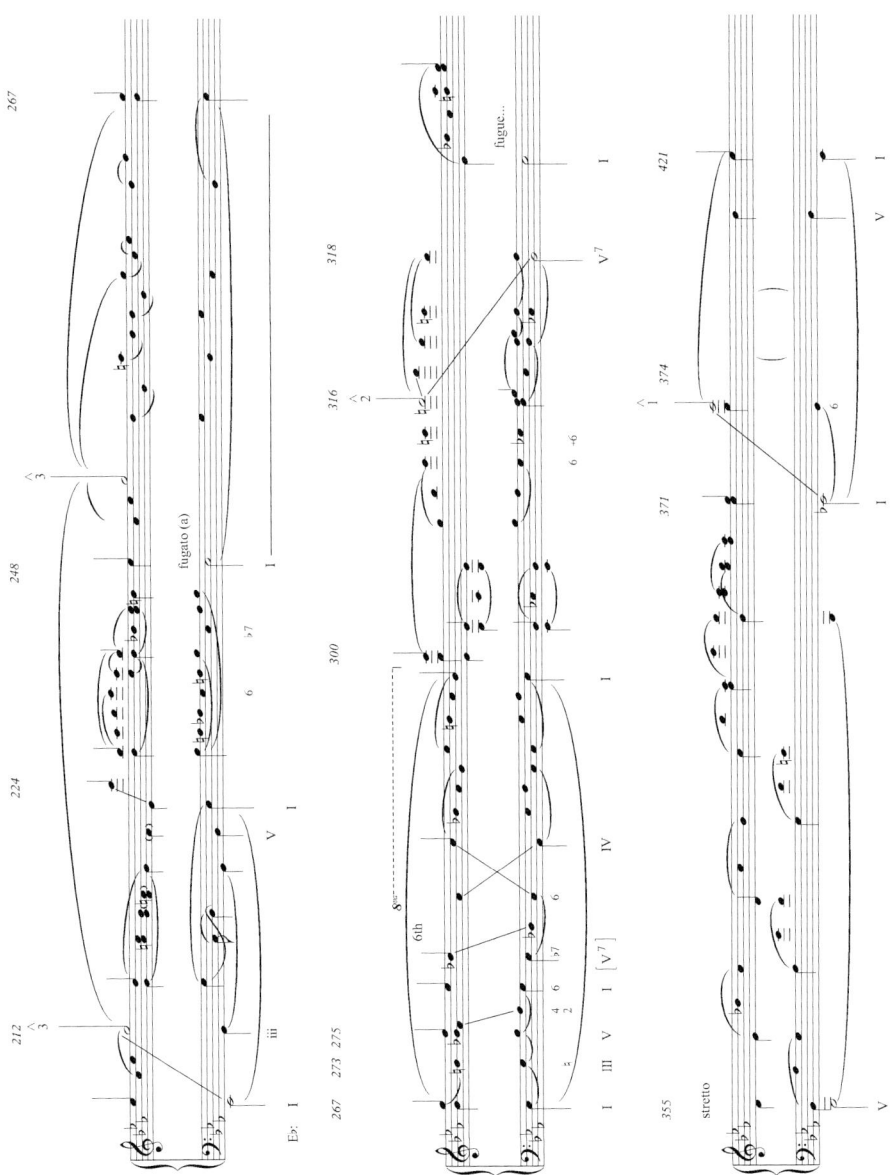

Example 2-16. Schumann (IV): Middleground graph of part IV

of G5/E♭, which is subsequently prolonged by a descending sixth in the passage beginning in bar 267. Arrival at the upper octave in bar 300 prepares the dramatic progression leading to the introduction of F6 ($\hat{2}$) via an augmented sixth chord (spelled again as a G♭7 chord) in bars 316–318. What follows is the fugue on the opening theme. Example 2-16 does not provide a detailed graph of the first portion of the fugue (the entrances),[12] but it does show the following stretto statements over a prolonged dominant leading back to the tonic at bar 371. The completion of the descent of the fundamental line to closure is shown to take place in the upper octave at bar 421 following the extended repetition of the earlier transitional passage beginning at bar 224.

An overview of the structure of this movement is given in Example 2-17. The division of the whole into parts is indicated by the vertical dotted lines. At the deepest level of the structure, iii supporting G5 progresses to iv supporting the upper neighbor of G5 at the beginning of the third part, and though this A♭5 moves up to B♭5 over the dominant, the notation suggests it is this A♭5 that ultimately leads to the primary tone at the beginning of the fourth part. At the middleground level iii is prolonged by a motion to its mediant before progressing to iv.

*

The return of the opening theme with its signature leap of a minor seventh as the subject of a fugue at the end of the quartet was an inspiration. Once you have experienced this conclusion, it is difficult to imagine a more effective ending or a more effective way of creating a sense of unity across considerable diversity. This is a grand gesture, but it is equally important to acknowledge less spectacular ways Schumann has created associations between as well as within movements. For example, once he employs G♭ within the first theme area of the first movement (as ♭VI in the key of the dominant), he brings it back later, first transformed as F♯ leading up to G three times in the a part of theme 2, the lead-in to the cello-viola duet, then later in the closing phrase as the bass note of an augmented sixth chord leading to the dominant of B♭. Much later Schumann creates a longer-range association by employing G♭ as the key of trio 1 in the third movement, again as ♭VI leading to the dominant in preparation for the return of the scherzo. The signature sounds of this scherzo are the ascending scales punctuated by the syncopated chords. Though very different in character, the idea associated with persona b in the narrative of the last movement is also based on scale segments. These statements are initially associated with E♭, the tonic, in a passage controlled by G minor / major, similar to the reference to E♭ within the G♭ area in the first movement. These references create another layer of association within the quintet, but we must be careful to interpret them within the contexts in which they have been placed.

---

12 The lack of full voice-leading graphs of the fugue and the earlier fugato should not be taken as diminishing their importance to this movement. The reason for these omissions is the difficulty of providing a clear voice-leading graph of a contrapuntal texture like a fugue in which the melodic line moves continually among the voices.

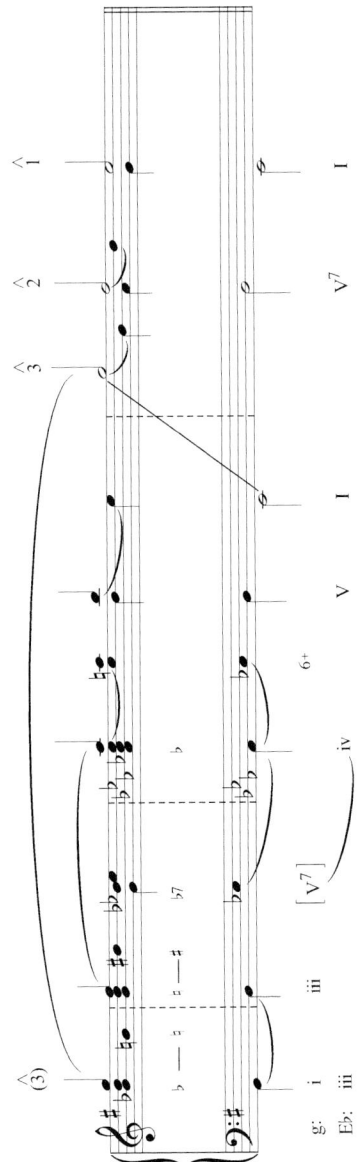

Example 2-17. Schumann (IV): Graph of the entire movement

Chapter III

Brahms. piano quintet, op. 34, in f minor

The genesis of the piano Quintet has been well documented. Brahms originally conceived of this work as a string sextet in 1862, and he shared this early version with both Clara Schumann and Joseph Joachim. Unfortunately, we do not have this early version of the work, but we do know that Brahms did receive comments from both Schumann and Joachim, some favorable, some critical, which he took seriously. This led to a complete remaking of the work as a Sonata for Two Pianos, originally completed in 1863-65 and later revised before publication in 1871. Meanwhile Brahms began working on yet another version for piano and string quartet, which was completed in 1865. It is this version that is generally accepted as Brahms's definitive statement of this material and the version frequently heard today in performance.

I. Allegro non troppo

The formal layout of this movement is outlined in Table 3-1, which shows the first theme area to have an a–b–a' design. A salient feature of the initial four-bar phrase is the neighbor-note pattern C–D♭–C, and our attention is drawn back to this D♭ immediately in the piano figuration of bar 5. This b section of the theme, which concludes with the emphatic cadence on the dominant in bar 11, leads to a more forceful and expanded statement of the opening idea. There is something unsettling about this b phrase, especially following the opening four bars, which suggest a quadruple hypermeter. In contrast, the b phrase is seven bars in length, and it contains conflicting hypermetric downbeats between piano and strings, initially six rather than four beats apart; however, the insistence of the strings in bars 10–11 restores some semblance of metric order. The following expanded statement of a with its clear reference to the C–D♭–C motive seems at first to re-establish the hypermeter, but only temporarily. The continuation, a most interesting passage that will be discussed in detail later, introduces G♭ (F♯) as the neighbor of F (bars 20–21), significant in that it foreshadows the key area of the second theme in the recapitulation (F♯ Minor) just as the motive at the original level, C–D♭–C, anticipates the key area of the second theme in the exposition (C♯ Minor). This phrase ends on a dominant ninth chord featuring the D♭, which prepares the following transition, where we hear this D♭ initially as displacing C, at the same time anticipating the modulation to D♭ Minor (vi), notated as C♯ Minor. Brahms has not only been careful in the detail of his writing to anticipate future events, but he has been equally fastidious in linking one idea to the next.

Theme 2, accompanied by a repeated triplet neighbor-note figure, has two contrasting parts, marked x and y in Table 3-1. The first part involves a descending arpeggiation G#5–E5–C#5 with each step decorated by its upper neighbor before reaching up to E6, the third of the prevailing tonic. By contrast, the y idea, a descending third incorporating a neighbor-note pattern, is registrally compact. The link between these contrasting parts is the triplet figure. The second statement of this theme then leads to a closing section in D♭ Major. Though this passage introduces some new elements, e.g., the dotted rhythmic figure, it also retains earlier features, like the decoration of F by G♭. It ends with a written-out deceleration approaching the final cadence, a doubling of the note values of the three-note pattern that is in conflict with the meter. The exposition is then repeated.

The development section is divided into four sections following a brief transition. The first, based on the opening motive of the movement, modulates to B♭ Minor (iv), and this key is continued through the next phrase, which is based on the transitional idea beginning in bar 23. The third part, based on the second theme, becomes rhythmically complex as it approaches the cadence in bar 150, completing the modulation to C Minor (v). At the deepest level of organization, the harmony has progressed from tonic (theme 1) to vi (theme 2) to iv, completing a descending third progression, to v. This last portion of the development, also based on the second theme, prolongs the dominant. What is somewhat unusual is that it is a statement of the b portion of theme 1 (bars 5–11) that leads to the major dominant, creating a formal overlap of development and recapitulation. The tonal recapitulation begins then in bar 173 with the a′ portion of theme 1.

The a′ phrase proceeds to the following transitional passage, where D♭ is heard initially as displacing C over F. This time the modulation is to F# Minor (enharmonically G♭ Minor =♭ii), a fifth lower than in the exposition for statements of theme 2 with its characteristic triplet accompaniment. The first statement progresses to the dominant in F# Minor, which becomes the pivot for the modulation back to F Minor; that is, the C# chord in bar 207 is reinterpreted as D♭ (VI) leading to the cadential six-four in F minor. The second statement begins on this six-four, proceeding initially to the tonic in bar 210, then confirming the return to the tonic via a cadential pattern leading to the downbeat of bar 218. The following passage, initially based on the motive associated with the second part of the second theme, proceeds to a cadence in the parallel major at bar 235, initiating the closing phrase and the following coda. Once again there is an overlap of formal units. The closing phrase ends with dominant harmony suspended over a tonic pedal, which resolves, at least initially, in the fifth bar of the coda. This contrapuntal passage leads to an extended statement of the b portion of theme 1, ending the movement convincingly in F Minor with a final reference to ♭ii, this time progressing through V to i.

The voice leading in this movement is set out in a series of foreground graphs,[1] beginning with Example 3-1, which provides the details of the first theme and the transition

---

[1] These graphs also provide information regarding longer-range connections, but I have included details intentionally because of the complexity of Brahms's style.

TABLE 3-1. BRAHMS (I): CHART OF THE FORMAL-TONAL DESIGN

EXPOSITION

Theme 1	a	1–4	f: i–V
	b	5–11	→ V
	a′	12–23	i–iv⁶–V⁹
Transition		23–33	i … c#: iv⁶–V
Theme 2, statement 1, x		35–38	c#(vi): i⁵⁻⁶ V,
	y	39–46	ii⁶/⁵ V …
statement 2, x		47–57	i … iv–V–i
	y	57–74	I… ⁷ iv–V–I
Closing Section		74–90	D♭ : I …iv⁶–V–I

DEVELOPMENT

Lead-in to bar 96	91–95	
Head motive of theme 1	96–122	mod. to B♭ mi. (iv)
Based on trans.	122–135	B♭ mi. (iv): i–V
Theme 2	137–150	i–mod to c(v)
Theme 2 – retrans. – theme 1 b	150–172	f: v … V

RECAPITULATION

Theme 1	a′	173–183	f: i–iv⁶–V⁹
Transition		184–194	i [ii V⁷]♭ii
Theme 2, statement 1, x		196–199	f# (♭ ii): i–V,
	y	200–208	ii⁶/⁵–V/f: VI–V
statement 2, x		208–218	f: V i…iv V I
	y	218–235	…iv⁺⁶/⁵ V⁷ I
Closing section		235–261	F: I–iv⁶–V–"I"

CODA

Contrapuntal treatment of idea based on theme 1	261–282	F: I
Return to beginning (b …)	283–299	f: →♭ii–V–iV⁷ i

to the second theme in the exposition. The primary tone A♭5 (3̂) is established immediately, and the initial four-bar idea (a) is shown to exhibit a lower-level interruption, which is embedded in the same motion across the first eleven bars. The voice leading of the b phrase involves an arpeggiation to C6 supported by an A♭ harmony followed by a linear descent to G5, the first three steps in parallel tenths with the bass. The rhythmic irregularity of this b phrase was noted above, though possibly the seven bars could be considered part of an eight-bar group by including the following bar, as shown in the example.

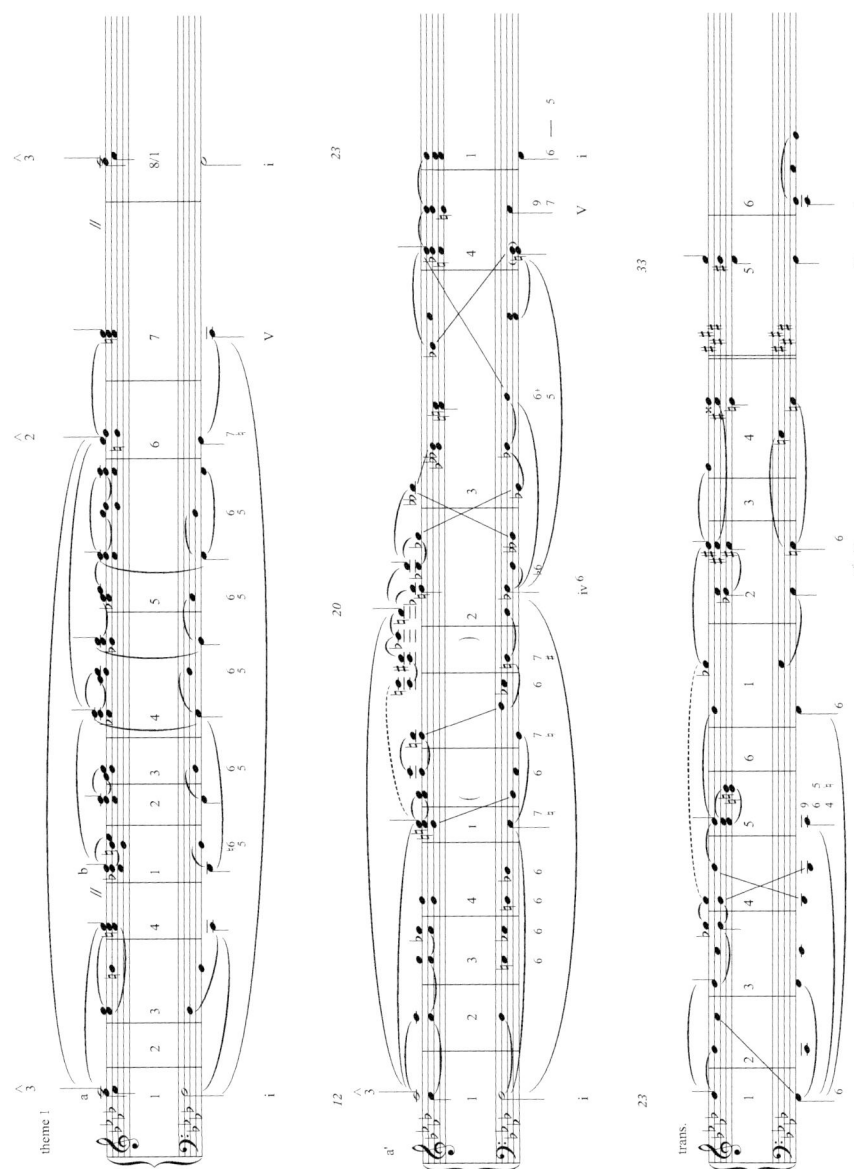

Example 3-1. Brahms (I): Foreground graph of theme 1 and transition (exposition)

The expanded restatement of the initial phrase is potentially confusing in the latter part because of Brahms's notation, which has been changed in the example to clarify the function of the chord progression. The underlying motion of bars 12–20 is a descending third $A\flat 5$–$G5$–$F5$, harmonized by i to iv^6, but with the last note stated an octave higher due to the content of bars 17–19, which are shown to be inserted into the hypermetric group. The second part of the phrase then prolongs the subdominant harmony on its way to the dominant ninth chord, first by a chromatic motion introducing the $G\flat$ minor chord, a brief suggestion of the key of the second theme, then by its transformation into an augmented sixth chord, which is subsequently prolonged by a chromatic voice exchange.[2] Arrival at the dominant ninth chord prepares the following transition, where $D\flat 5$, the ninth of the dominant, is retained as displacement of $C5$, but at the same time preparing the modulation to $D\flat$ Minor.

The second theme opens with the descending arpeggiation $G\sharp 5$–$E5$–$C\sharp 5$, each step decorated by its upper neighbor, suggesting that the structure of this theme will likely be a descending fifth, but then the melody reaches up to $E6$, locally $\hat{3}$, which, like the opening idea, leads to a local interruption in the fourth bar. As indicated by the longer slur in Example 3-2, this motion is embedded in the longer-range progression to the dominant in bars 41–42. The varied repetition of bars 39–42, which emphasizes VI, delays resolution to the tonic. This statement of the theme completes the motion to local closure, internal to which the third scale degree is transferred to the upper octave, harmonized by VI, followed by an embellished descent in that octave harmonized by the major tonic in first inversion, propelling the music forward to the standard cadential pattern supporting the descent in the lower octave.

A separate graph of the second part of the theme (bars 57–74) featuring its characteristic neighbor-note motive is provided in Example 3-3. The main structural feature of this passage is the prolongation of the $C\sharp$ major harmony and the process of reaching up to the seventh in bars 67–68, which leads to iv–V in the following two bars. Arrival at the local tonic, now spelled as a $D\flat$ chord, is delayed by the varied repetition of bars 69–70 (iv–V), where the subdominant is extended across two bars.

The graphic notation in example 3-4 has been changed to focus on the overall motion of this closing phrase without becoming mired in too much detail. The phrase opens with a sweeping gesture reaching up to $F5$, which is repeated a third higher four bars later. The intervening progression in descending thirds represents the combined motion of the dotted rhythmic idea moving from strings to piano (bars 76–78); this too is repeated a third higher four bars later. Beginning in bar 82 each step represented by the descending thirds in parallel tenths is embellished by its own third: $G\flat$ ($F E\flat$)-F ($E\flat D\flat$)-$E\flat$, etc. The climax of the phrase is reached at bar 85 at the iv^6 chord featuring $G\flat$, and it is at this point that Brahms decelerates going into the final cadence by doubling the value of the notes in the three-note pattern. Simultaneously there is a gradual expansion of the intervals between the notes of the pattern.

---

2 This voice exchange shows the underlying norm, which is altered by the addition of a bass a third below.

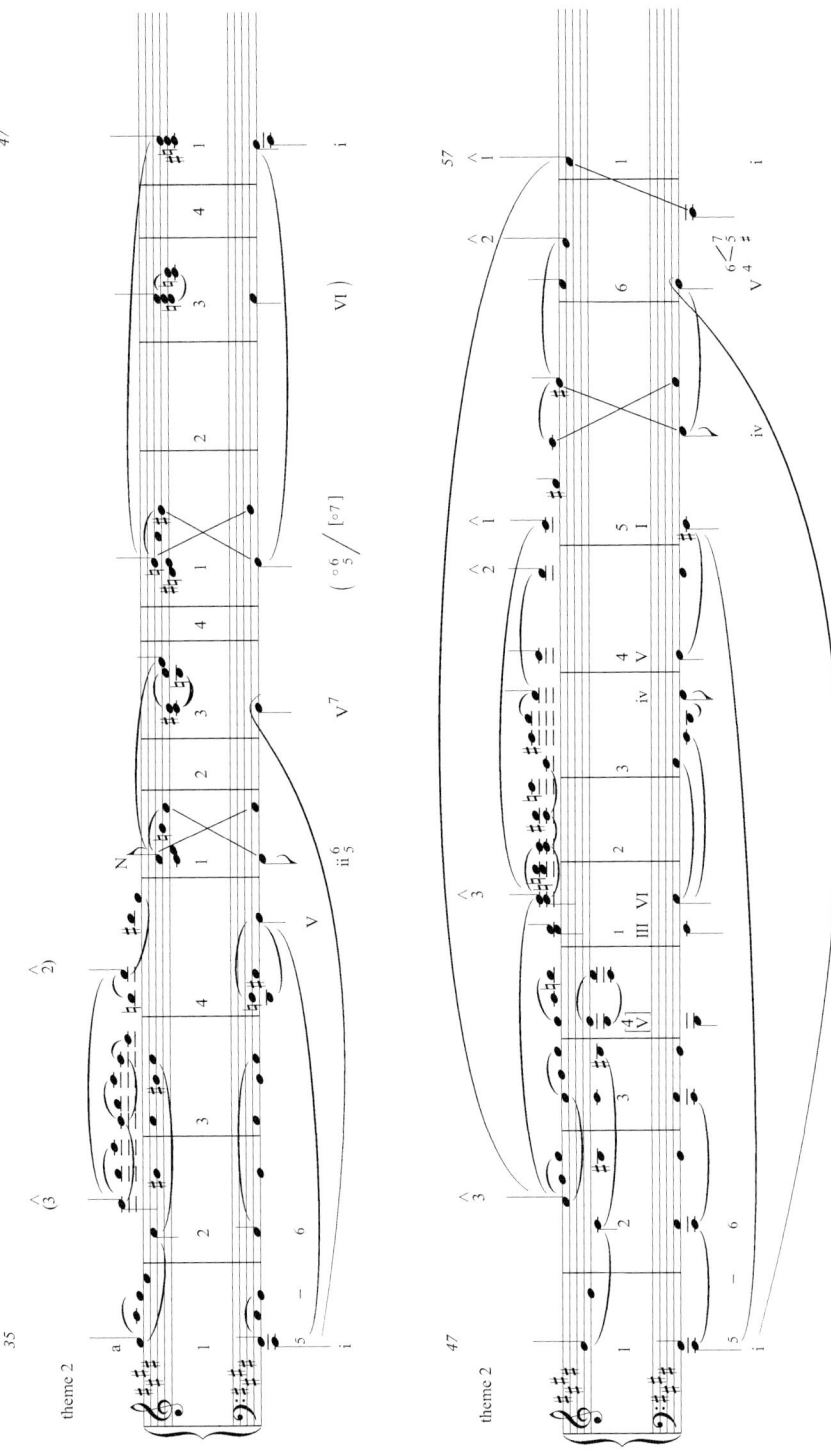

Example 3-2. Brahms (I): Foreground graph of theme 2 (exposition)

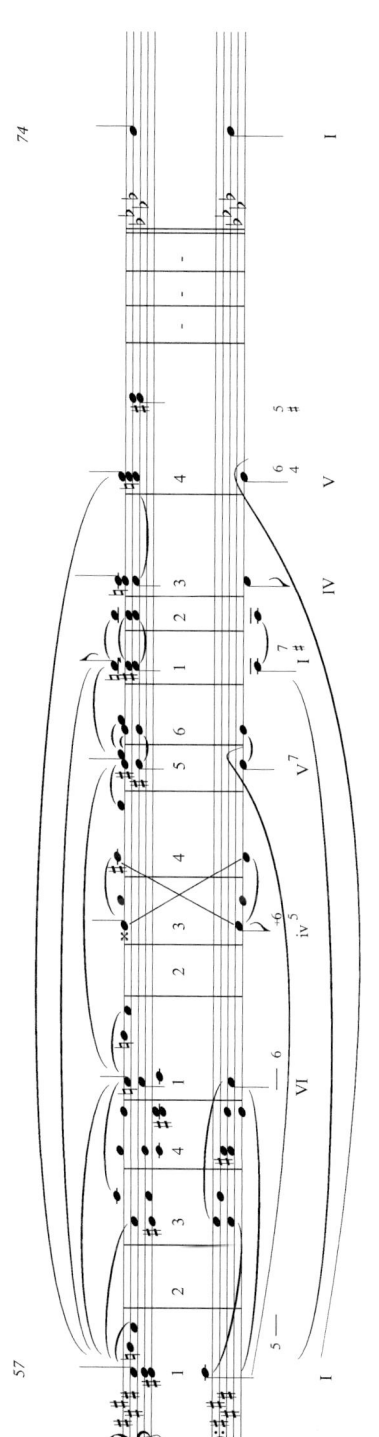

Example 3-3. Brahms (I): Foreground graph of the second part of theme 2 (exposition)

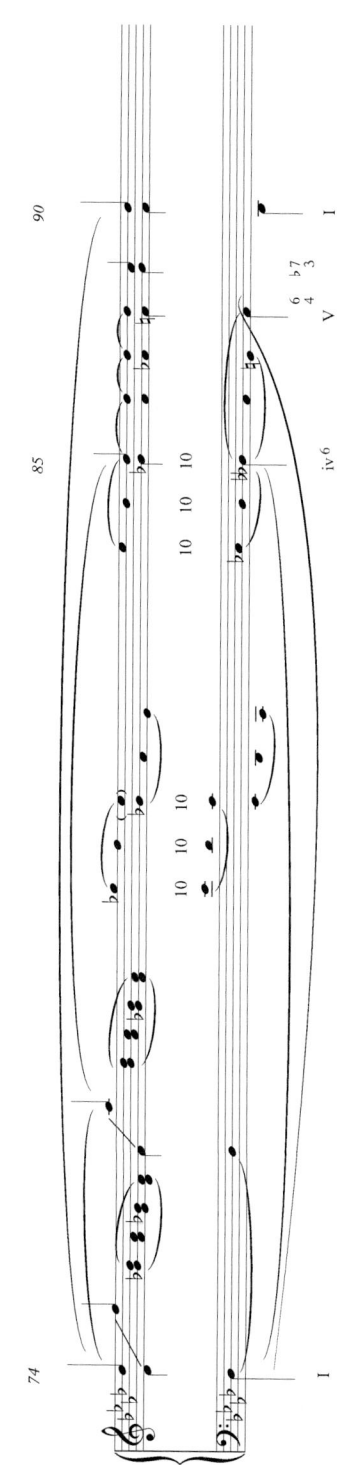

Example 3-4. Brahms (I): Middleground graph of bars 74–90

When Brahms adds the seventh to the D♭ chord at the very beginning of the development, it seems we are headed toward G♭. The music does get there several measures later (bar 108), notated as an F♯ major chord, but the D♭ⁿ⁷ chord is followed immediately by G⁷ supporting the first statement of an idea based on the head motive of the opening phrase. The meaning of this chord is not clear: Is it projecting the eventual arrival at the dominant, as the preceding chord suggests G♭, or is it potentially an augmented sixth chord with E♯ spelled as F? The latter possibility seems to evaporate when the seventh is displaced by the octave (bar 100), after which G5 is resolved to the octave of the F♯ harmony at bar 108. As suggested in Example 3-5, a middleground graph of the development section, the G⁷ chord does resolve to the F♯ harmony as if it were an augmented sixth chord. The following few measures, which present no new problems of interpretation, have been omitted from the graph to highlight the connection between the F♯ chord and the G♭ chord at bar 119, which then leads to the cadential progression completing the modulation to B♭ Minor (iv). As was noted above, the second part of the development (indicated on the graph by 2. above the staff) prolongs the subdominant. The main structural features of this section are the arpeggiation from the inner voice back to F5 and its prolongation by its upper neighbor G♭. Musically this passage grows in intensity, reaching its climactic point in bar 133.

The third part of the development, based on theme 2, is announced by its characteristic triplet accompaniment figure. It opens with a four-bar idea represented in the graph by the descending bass motion of a third B♭–G♭ supporting a melodic motion from F5 to F♭6. This idea is then repeated a half step higher, as indicated by the brackets above the bass thirds. It seems this second statement is extraneous in terms of the overall motion of the passage, which becomes clear in the following measures with the 8–♭7 motion over A♭ (next two measures) and the following 10–7 sequence, which leads to the II⁷–V⁷–I cadence on v. The final approach to the cadence is complex rhythmically with the upper parts continuing with a rhythmic pattern congruent with the meter, while the bass pattern is delayed by half a beat, a conflict that is resolved on the downbeat of bar 150, initiating part 4. From a structural perspective the important features of this last part are the arpeggiation to the covering C6 and the change from minor to major dominant. But it is left to the following statement of the b phrase from the first theme to lead the covering C6 down to G5/V to complete the motion to interruption of the fundamental line.

A middleground graph of the entire movement to the point of interruption is given in Example 3-6. This graph requires little explanation beyond what has already been noted. The main structural features of the exposition are the prolongation of the primary tone A♭5 and the modulation from i (theme 1) to vi/VI (theme 2). The development progresses to iv, completing the long-range descending third progression, then to V supporting the interruption. At the deepest level this is a common paradigm for a sonata movement in the minor mode,[3] the only non-standard feature being the delay of the structural dominant until part b of the first theme has been stated.

---

3 See, for example, the first movement of Schubert's Symphony in B Minor (D759).

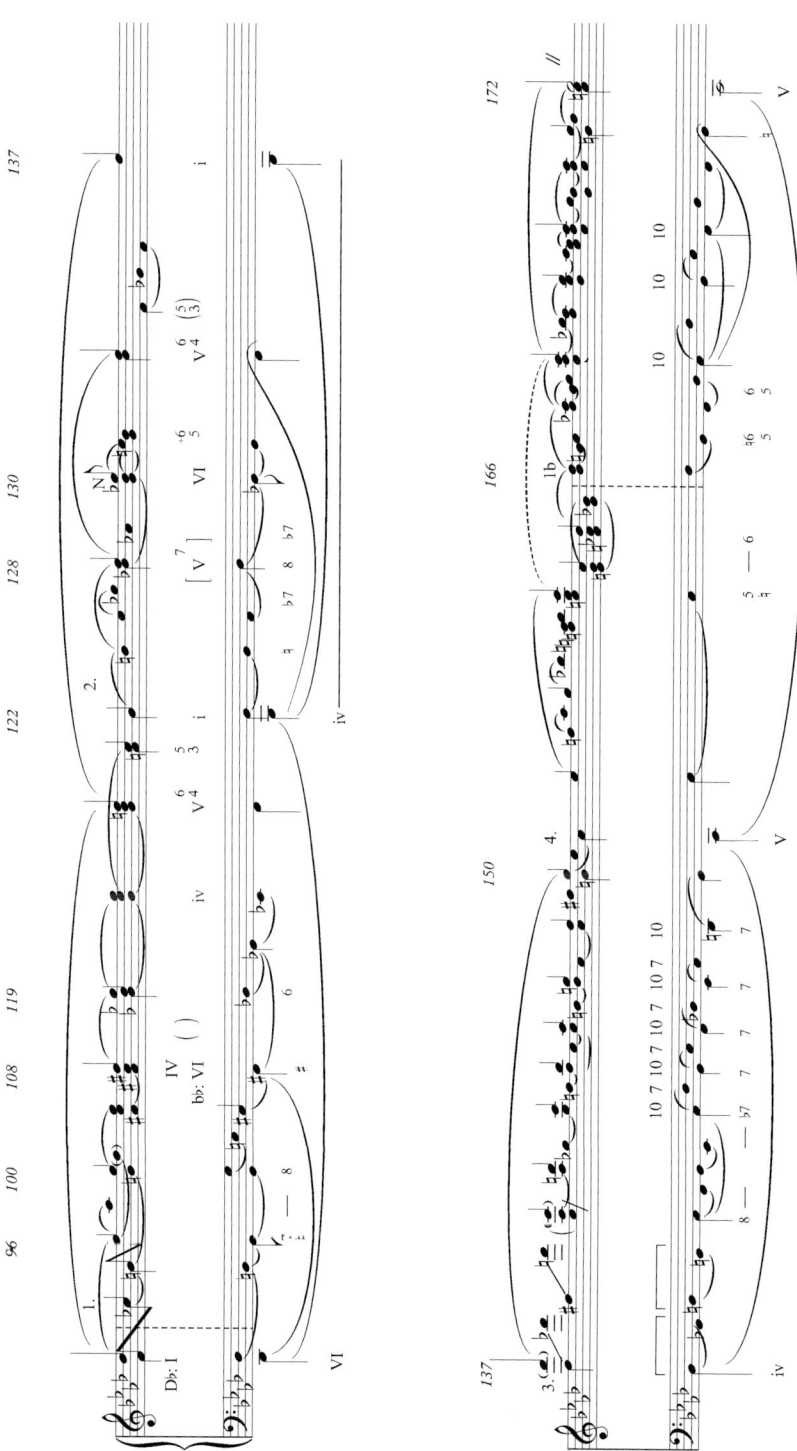

Example 3-5. Brahms (I): Foreground graph of the development section

Bars 173–183, the initial phrase of the tonal return, is a varied repetition of bars 12–22, ending, as before, on a dominant ninth chord. In the exposition we hear the following chord as a tonic with D♭ displacing C, but here in the recapitulation the transitional passage begins with a ninth chord on F, that is, with G♭ displacing F. As shown in Example 3-7, this ninth chord on F is first articulated by the cello, then repeated four bars later by violin 1 leading to ii⁷(written as an A♭ chord) – V, preparing the modulation to F♯ Minor.

The two statements of theme 2 follow. After the initial descending arpeggiation of a fifth, the melodic line reaches up to A5, scale degree 3, which leads to $\hat{2}$ /V in the fourth bar. The second part of the theme then progresses to the dominant, which becomes the pivot for the modulation back to F Minor, as indicated in Example 3-8. The second statement begins on a six-four leading to the tonic in bar 210 for a statement of the theme that will proceed to local closure. This statement is more complex, involving two octaves. By the time A4 has been transferred to A5, the harmony has changed to VI, leading, as shown, to the cadential pattern supporting the descent of the melodic line to closure in the upper octave. However, the bass note at this point of melodic closure (downbeat of bar 216), is A natural, propelling the music through this point to a second "attempt" to achieve closure in the lower octave. Brahms avoids a strong closing statement here, the first of several times he will do so, in this instance by arriving early at the tonic harmony.

Example 3-9 is in two parts. The first represents the second part of theme 2, second statement (bars 218–235). An important feature of the first few bars of this passage is the prolongation of F by G♭, a fundamental ingredient in this movement paralleling the displacement of C by D♭. Following the change of key signature, the dominant is introduced by an augmented sixth chord prolonged by a voice exchange.[4] The prolongation of this dominant also employs G♭ ; then, buried in an inner part (cello) there is an embellished statement of the structural descent, where arrival at the tonic has been delayed by a three-bar insertion, an expansion of the preceding two bars. The voice leading of a portion of the closing phrase, which is considerably extended, is shown below. Here the descending third A4-G4-F4 and later C5–B♭4–A4 represent the dotted rhythmic idea characteristic of the first part of this passage. Beginning in bar 244, the pattern of descending thirds is stated off beat against the meter, then the values of the pattern are doubled as if to head into a cadence. But Brahms does not continue as he had at the end of the exposition. Instead, beginning in bar 251, he continues to exploit the interaction of pattern versus meter, piano versus strings, and then he changes the pattern to quadruple / duple against the underlying pulse articulated by the cello and piano (left hand). In short, this passage is rhythmically unsettled,[5] which continues into the section marked *poco sostenuto* (bar 261 ff.). This part

---

4 This same chord is sounded at the very beginning of the development section spelled as a D♭ ⁷ chord leading some measures later to a G♭/F♯ chord. Here the C♭ is spelled and treated as a B natural leading to the dominant.

5 The manipulation of rhythm versus meter as the music approaches an important cadence or, like here, delaying the cadence, seems to be a hallmark of Brahms's style.

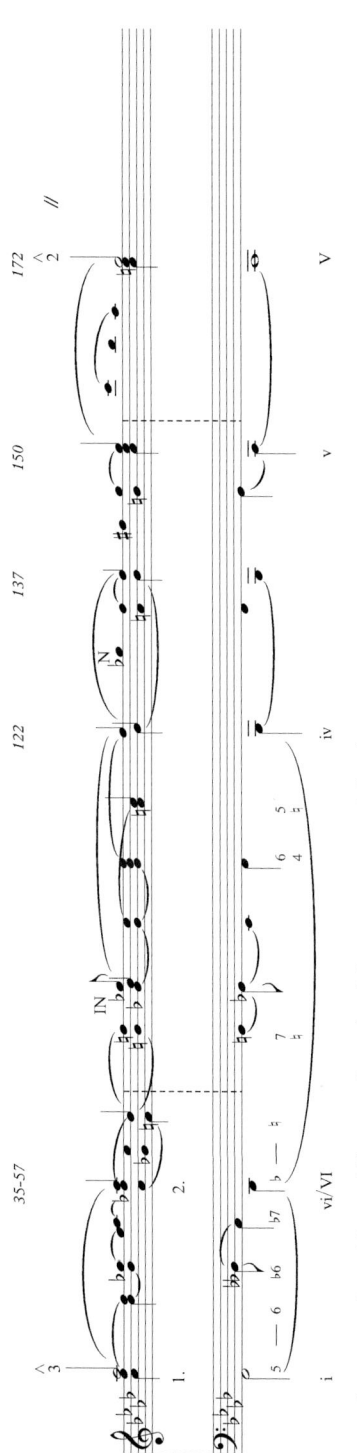

Example 3-6. Brahms (I): Middleground graph of the exposition and development

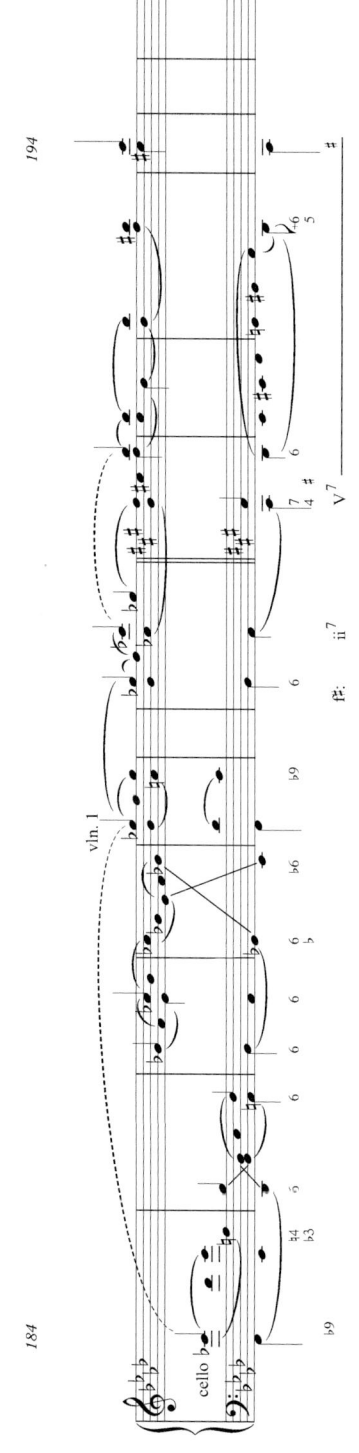

Example 3-7. Brahms (I): Foreground graph of theme 1 and transition (recapitulation)

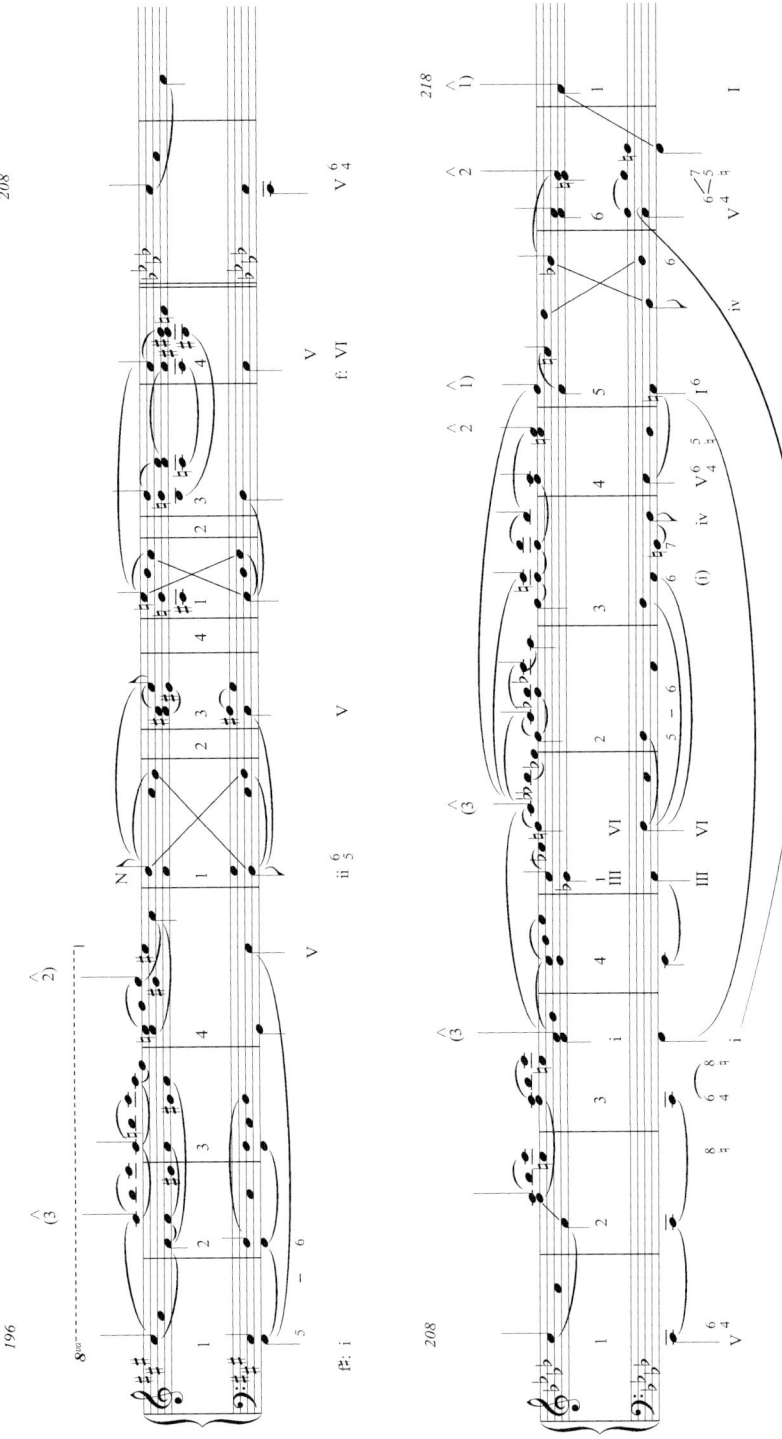

Example 3-8. Brahms (I): Foreground graph of theme 2 (recapitulation)

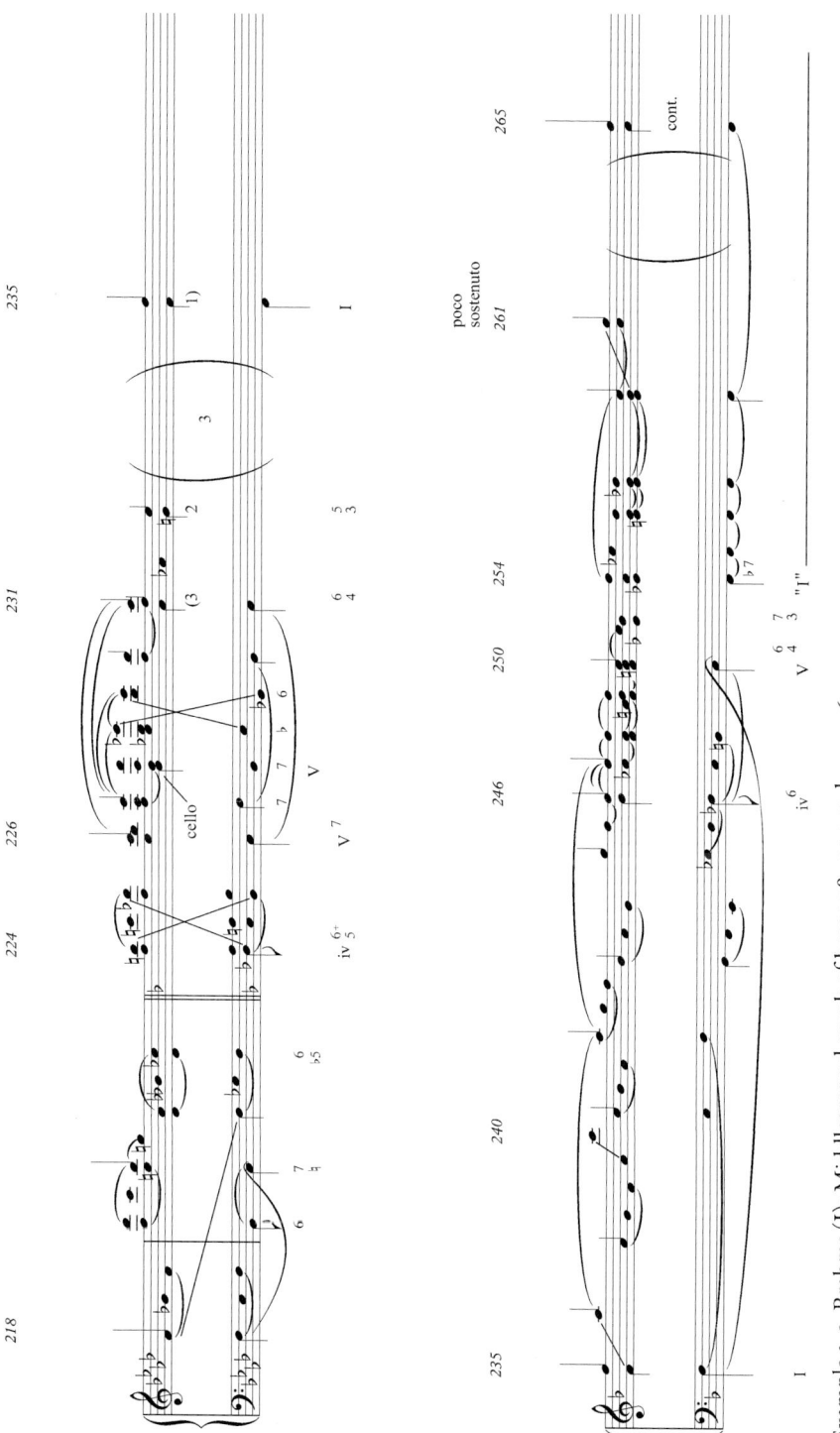

Example 3-9. Brahms (I): Middleground graph of bars 218–235 and 235–265

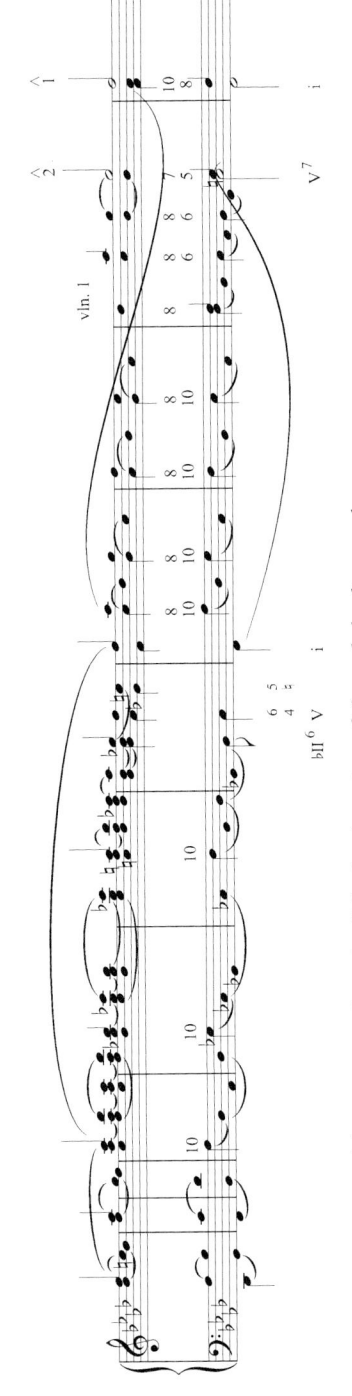

Example 3-10. Brahms (I): Foreground graph of the final portion of the coda leading to closure

of the extended passage is not represented in the graph; it delays the build-up to and entrance of the final statement of the b phrase and its continuation to a grand conclusion.

The final portion of the coda is represented in Example 3-10. As in the preceding statements of this material, the melody arpeggiates to C6 supported by an A♭ chord, after which the top line begins its descent to F5, initially in parallel tenths with the bass. However, this descent to closure is through ♭2, a final recall of G♭ and to the key of the second theme in the recapitulation. It then falls to the following phrase to bring the fundamental structure to full closure.

II. Andante, un poco adagio

The design of this movement is ternary plus coda, and it features the piano prominently, though the strings do contribute to melodic statements in the B and A′ sections. The first section has the character of a lullaby with its repetitive rhythmic figure, limited range and lower dynamic level, though the music does reach a brief climactic point in bar 16. It is written in the key of A♭ Major, and the transition leads to F♭ Major (♭VI), notated by Brahms as E Major. In contrast to the first part, the B section employs a wider dynamic and pitch range, and it is more complex rhythmically, employing triplets and 3 against 2. The music then returns to the lullaby, the only change being the statement of the second phrase by violin 1, opening the range to the upper octave. The coda returns initially to the character of the B section, then tapers off to a quiet ending with a recall of the close of the A section.

The A section consists of two phrases, an antecedent and a consequent, plus a transition. As indicated in Example 3-11, the initial phrase establishes the primary tone C4 ($\hat{3}$) at the very beginning and progresses to B♭/V in the fourth bar, a lower-level interruption. The next four bars prolong B♭/V, during which C♭ is introduced in passing, a coloration not only suggesting the minor mode but also a foreshadowing of the central role of that pitch (B natural) in the next section. Rather than return to the tonic in bar 9, the dominant is extended for another four bars, indicated in the graph as a parenthetical insertion, a delay in reaching the goal.[6] This sitting on the dominant – motion without motion – contributes to the lullaby character of this section. The consequent phrase then completes the motion to local closure, first in bar 23, then confirmed four bars later.[7] In this phrase the music reaches up to D♭5, the upper neighbor of the primary tone, first supported by IV, then as the seventh of the dominant. The subsequent prolongation introduces several chromatic elements that anticipate the modulation to F♭/E, which is accomplished by a standard cadential pattern.

An important feature of the B section is the repetition of a pitch motive B–A–G♯–F♯, statements of which are highlighted in Example 3-12 by brackets. This idea is stated initially in bars 35–36 as an inner part in the triplet figure below the repeated Bs, but it is then repeated immediately in the upper octave, this time with G natural rather than G sharp. A varied and expanded repetition of this phrase begins in bar 43 with the repetition of the triplets and the descending fourth sounding below a sustained B5.[8] This is followed by two additional statements below a sustained B4, again with G natural replacing G sharp. These two statements of the motive are embedded within a descending fifth leading to the cadence in bar 55. This motivic idea is stated again in the transition, now transposed in an inner part below a transfer of E4 to E5 in preparation of the following chromatic descent to D♭/V to reintroduce the primary tone at the beginning of the A′ section.

The repetition of bars 1–8 at the beginning of the A′ section is not included in Example 3-13. What follows is not a statement just of the consequent phrase by violin 1, but a statement of both the antecedent and consequent phrases, bars 83–94 and 94–104. The first leads to interruption in bar 87, and then $\hat{3}$ is re-introduced in bar 95 by its upper neighbor D natural as part of a G major chord, as in bar 12. The consequent phrase is the parallel of bars 13–23, leading to closure in bar 104 via an implied B♭4. The bottom system of Example 3-13 represents the essential voice leading of the coda. Of particular interest here is the emphasis given to G♭ leading to F, a reference to the first movement superimposed on the descent to A♭.

Example 3-14 provides an overview of the movement, in which the key of the B section has been notated as F♭ to show its function within the whole. The A section exhibits a

---

6 This insertion ends with an implied G major chord, so the return to the tonic also carries the impression of a deceptive progression in C Minor.

7 The confirming four bars (24–27) have not been included in the graph.

8 Example 3-12 is designed to show bars 43–55 is an expansion of bars 35–42.

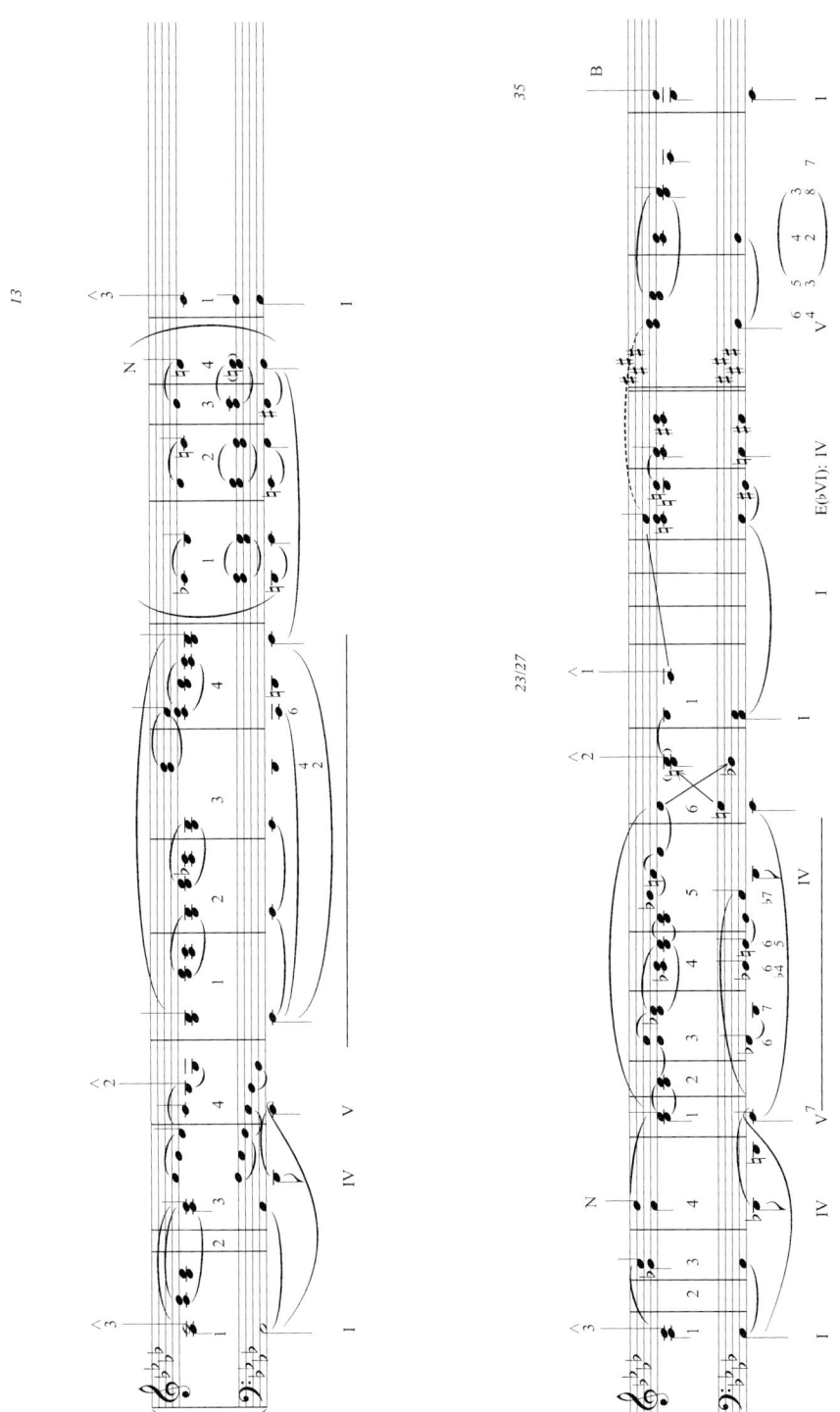

Example 3-11. Brahms (II): Foreground graph of the A section

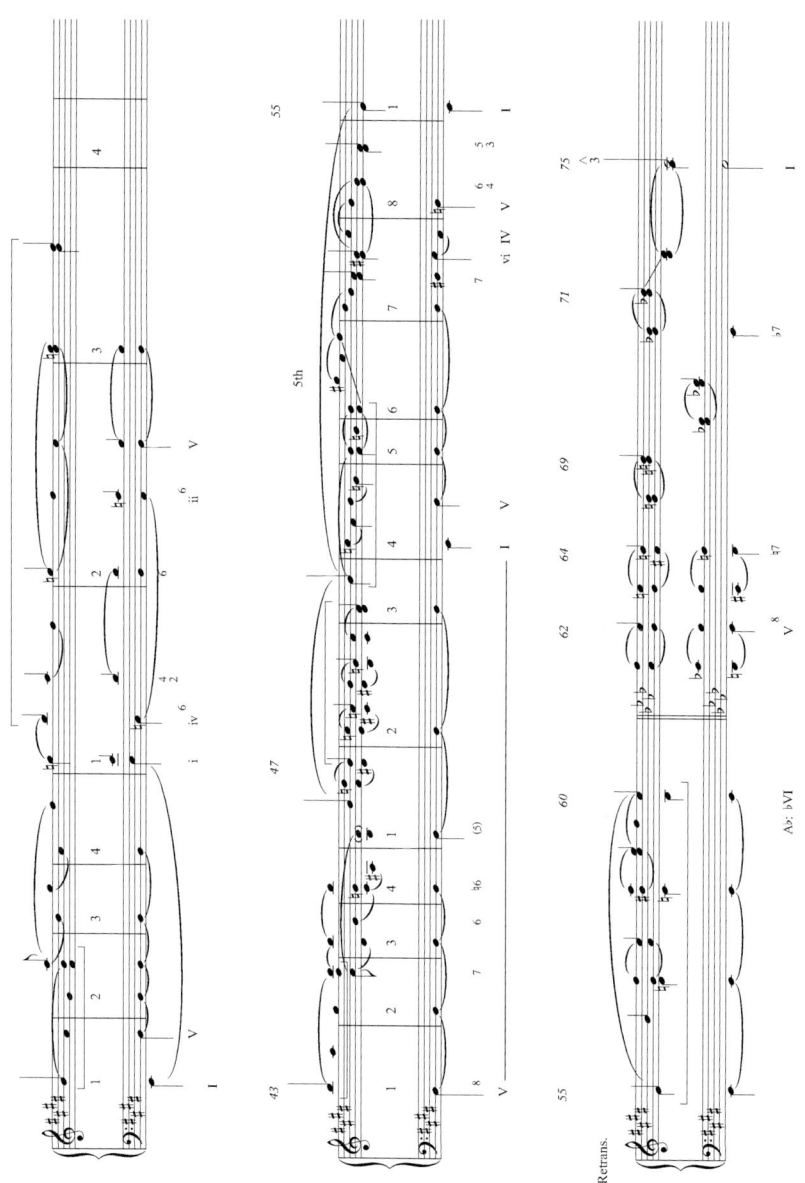

Example 3-12. Brahms (II): Foreground graph of the B section and retransition

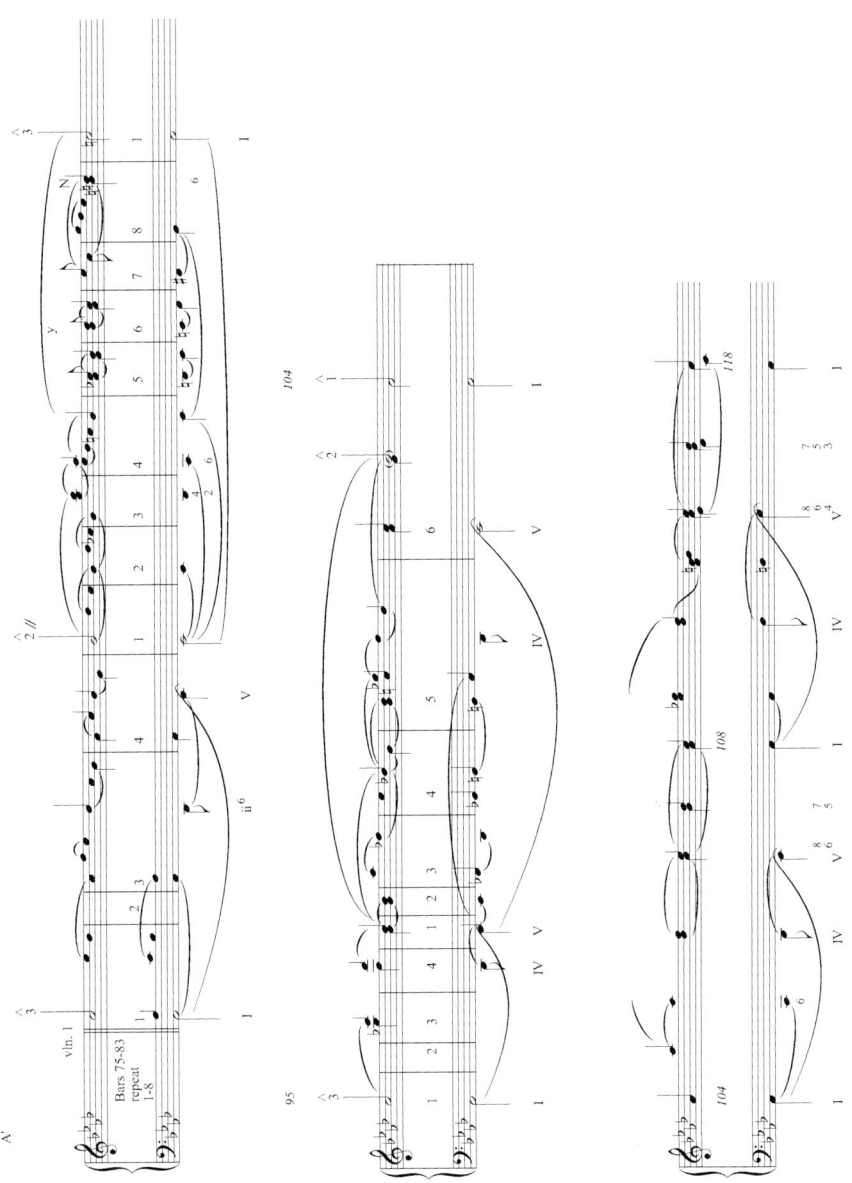

Example 3-13. Brahms (II): Foreground graph of the A' section and coda

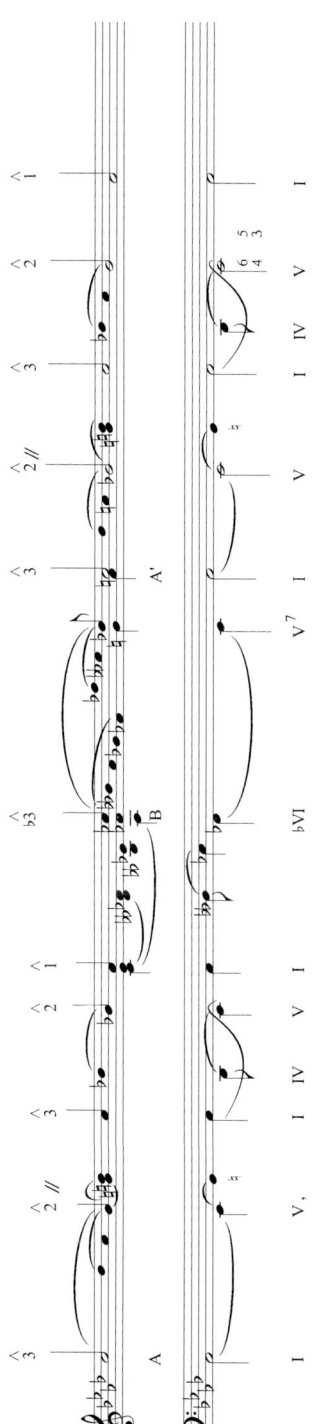

Example 3-14. Brahms (II): Middleground graph of the entire movement

lower-level interruption, a middleground parallel of the fundamental structure, and the B section is shown to prolong $C^\flat$ ($\flat$3) before C natural is reintroduced by its upper neighbor.

III. Scherzo, allegro

The form of the scherzo can be divided conveniently into five parts as outlined in Table 3-2. The first consists of the initial statements of the three main ideas of the movement: a) the opening syncopated idea over a tonic pedal; b) the repeated-note rhythmic pattern; and c) the chorale. This part ends with a recall of the a idea accompanied by the driving rhythmic pattern associated with c, the chorale. The key of this first part is C Minor / Major (chorale), and each of its phrases ends on the dominant. Part II is a partial restatement of the preceding part, again with phrases ending on the dominant. The restatement of the a idea concludes on II♯ as if to lead to the key of the dominant, but the following statement of b concludes on a $B^\flat$ chord, the dominant of $E^\flat$ Minor, the key of the following fugue (part III), which interrupts the varied restatement of ideas. Once again, the points of arrival in this fugue fall on the dominant. Part IV then begins where Part II concluded, with a statement of the chorale in $E^\flat$ Major followed by an extended section based on a that leads to closure in bar 158. The final part (V), based on b, functions like a coda, concluding with a syncopated idea that ends the movement with the repeated melodic gesture $D^\flat$–C (phrygian 2), a reference – now in a different context – to the main motivic component of the first movement.

The influence of Bach on this movement is clear, not only the inclusion of a chorale and fugue, but also the modal quality that pervades the movement. Similar to what was observed in the second movement of the Schumann Quintet, Brahms ends the movement by emphasizing the subdominant to conclude the movement on a major chord, indeed elaborated by $^\flat$II. It seems he has prepared this idea throughout by ending phrases on the dominant. That is, the major tonic at the end is approached as if it were the dominant of the subdominant, though, of course, it isn't that; it is the tonic, just as the major chord that ends many of Bach's modal works is the tonic.

A remarkable feature of this movement is the care taken by Brahms to link one idea to the next. The opening phrase features $A^\flat$ as displacement of G, a link to the previous movement. As shown in the top system of Example 3-15, this initial idea ends with the descending fourth C6–$B^\flat$5–$A^\flat$5–G5, marked with a bracket and identified as motive x. This is followed by the rhythmic idea (b), here featuring repeated Gs. Twice the repeated note is elaborated, first by the figure G–$A^\flat$–G–$E^\flat$–F–G, identified by a curly bracket and y, then by G–C–$B^\flat$–G–$E^\flat$–F–G, a gesture that combines features of both x and y.[9] This

---

9 This idea, an elaboration of the descending tetrachord C–$B^\flat$–$A^\flat$–G, where G is approached from below rather than via $A^\flat$, is reminiscent of the latter half of the opening idea from the final movement of the Schumann Quintet (see Example 2-13 and the accompanying text), suggesting a subtle tribute by Brahms to this important earlier work.

TABLE 3-2. BRAHMS (III): CHART OF THE FORMAL-TONAL DESIGN

SCHERZO

I. Initial Statement of Ideas			
	a. sync./+4/3 idea	1–13	c: i → V
	b. rhythmic idea	13–21	→ V
	c. chorale	22–38	I → V
	a/c	39–46	+4/3 → V
II. Partial Restatement			
	a	47–57	→ II#
	b	57–67	e♭: → V
III. Fugue on b		67–109	e♭: → V
IV. Remainder of Restatement			
	c	109–124	E♭: → V
	a/c	125–157	c: i–♭II–V–i
V. Final Section			
	b	158–176	c: i–[V⁷] iv–I
	b/a	177–193	II♭ ⁶–I

TRIO

A			
	a	193–210	C: I–V
	a′	210–225	I–V
B			
	b	226–233	V
	b′	233–241	V
A′	a″	241–261	I♭ ⁷–IV/iv …I

is followed by a clear statement of y by the viola, followed by the chorale, which opens with a major key version of y. Overall this phrase descends a fourth, a transposed version of x, and the following phrase then states x at the original pitch level, but now in the major mode. Despite the strong emphasis given to G throughout this first part, the primary tone is identified as E♭5 ($\hat{3}$), a decision made after examination of the entire movement.

The restatement of a confirms the primary tone as E♭5, which then leads to D5/II#, a temporary goal that is prolonged by a motion to the upper octave (see Example 3-16). The following statement of the repeated pitch idea (b) progresses from D5 to F5 to A♭5 with each step decorated either by y or x/y, as shown in the graph. The final gesture concludes with a further statement of y leading to the dominant in E♭ Minor preparing for the fugue. Though this fugue occupies a central position in the movement, it is parenthetical from a structural perspective, delaying the statement of the chorale, and for this among other

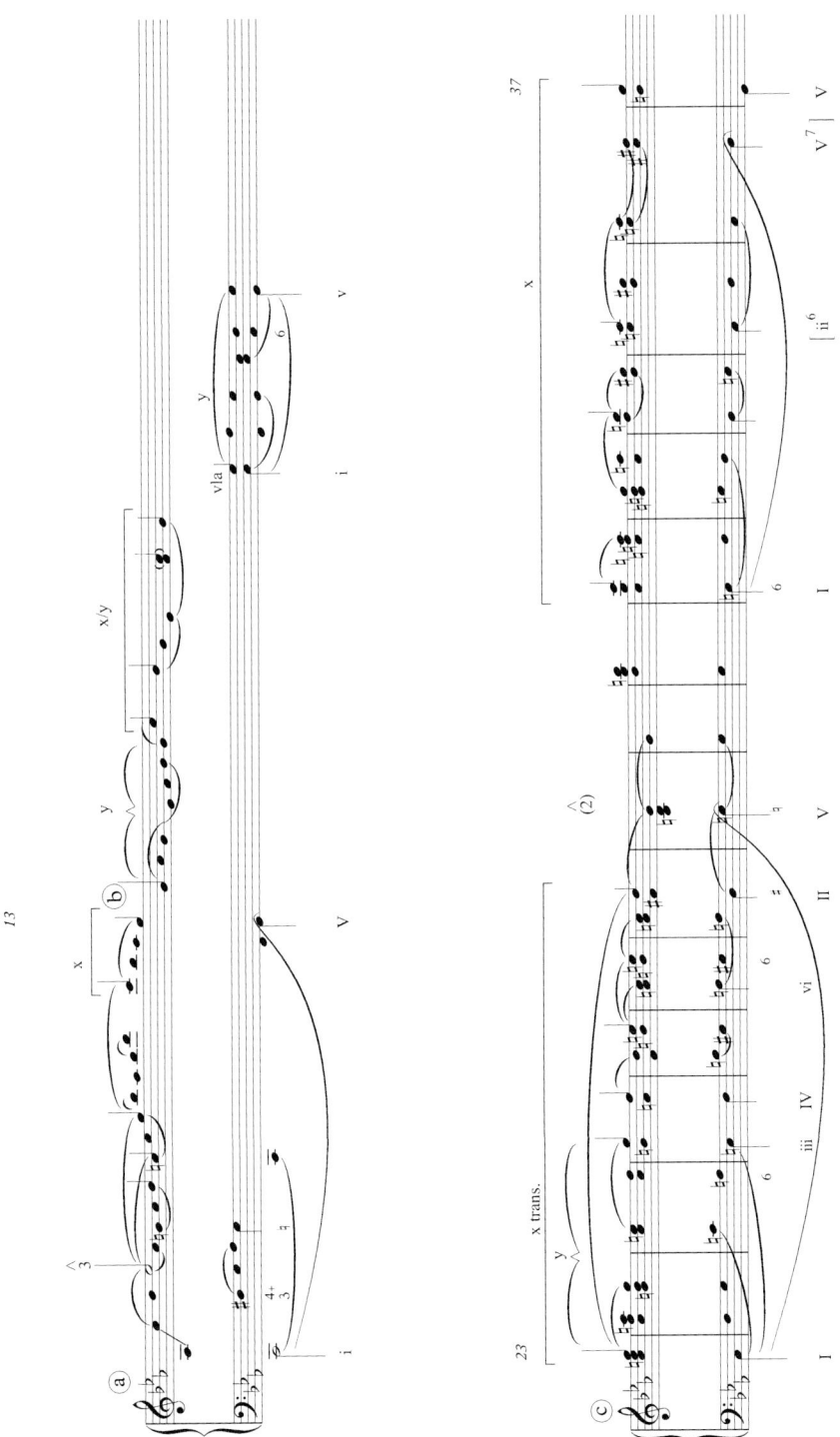

Example 3-15. Brahms (III): Graph of the scherzo, part 1

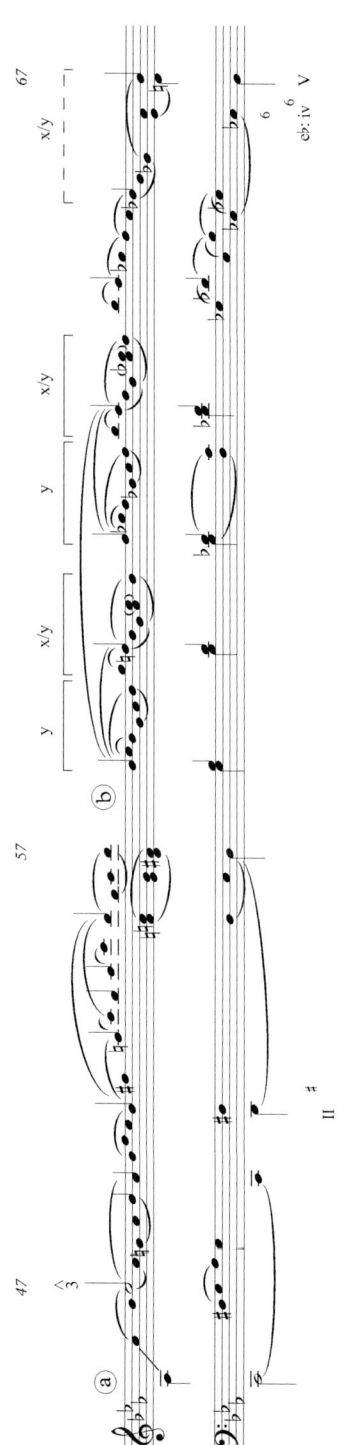

Example 3-16. Brahms (III): Graph of the scherzo, part 2

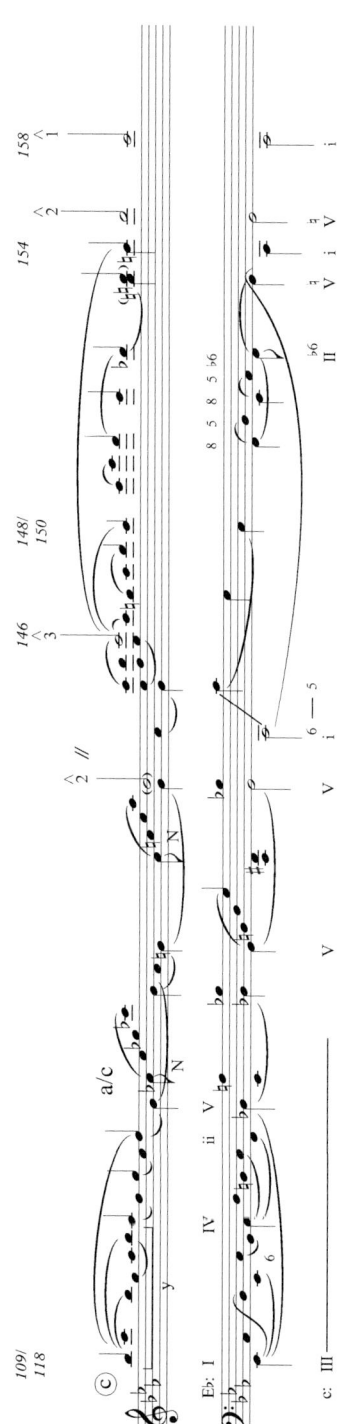

Example 3-17. Brahms (II): Graph of the scherzo, part 4

89

reasons no graph of it has been provided. However, pertinent to the preceding discussion, it is interesting to note that this part ends with very clear and forceful (*ff*) statements of motive y and its variant x/y in bars 100–109 over the dominant in E♭ Minor.

Part IV begins with two statements of the chorale phrase in the key of E♭ Major (III) progressing from I to V, the first by the piano and the second by violin 1. As indicated in Example 3-17, this idea opens with a statement of motive y, which is embedded in the descending fourth E♭5–A♭5–G5–F5, a transposition of motive x. The continuation first prolongs B♭4 by its upper neighbor C♭5 harmonized by an embellishing augmented sixth chord, a feature of the opening idea, and this gesture is then repeated a third lower on the dominant in the tonic key. Overall, this section has progressed from III to V supporting an implied D5 and interruption of the fundamental structure. This motion prepares the return to the tonic and the opening idea in bar 144, followed two bars later by the re-statement of the primary tone and an initial descent to closure, which is embedded within two longer-range motions, the first leading through II♭6–V–i (bar 154) and the second achieving closure through D6/V to C6/i.

A middleground graph of the scherzo, excluding the coda, is provided in Example 3-18. At the deepest level Part I progresses from i to V supporting a lower-level interruption. Part II re-establishes $\hat{3}$/I before leading first to II♯, then to B♭, V of E♭ Minor (iii) for the fugue and then the chorale in the parallel major. The continuation leads to the dominant and to an implied interruption. Overall, the movement has progressed from i through iii/III to V supporting a motion from $\hat{3}$ to $\hat{2}$. The return to the opening material at bar 144 leads to a restatement of $\hat{3}$/i, which now progresses to closure of the fundamental structure.

The coda, initially based on the driving rhythm of the b idea, leads to the subdominant in bar 167, which is subsequently prolonged until its resolution to the major tonic harmony at bar 176. This is followed by an embellishment of the major tonic by II♭6, then at the very end by the melodic gesture D♭–C, which Brahms hammers into our ears 5 times. A very forceful statement at the end of a coda that has raced along *fortissimo* from the very beginning.

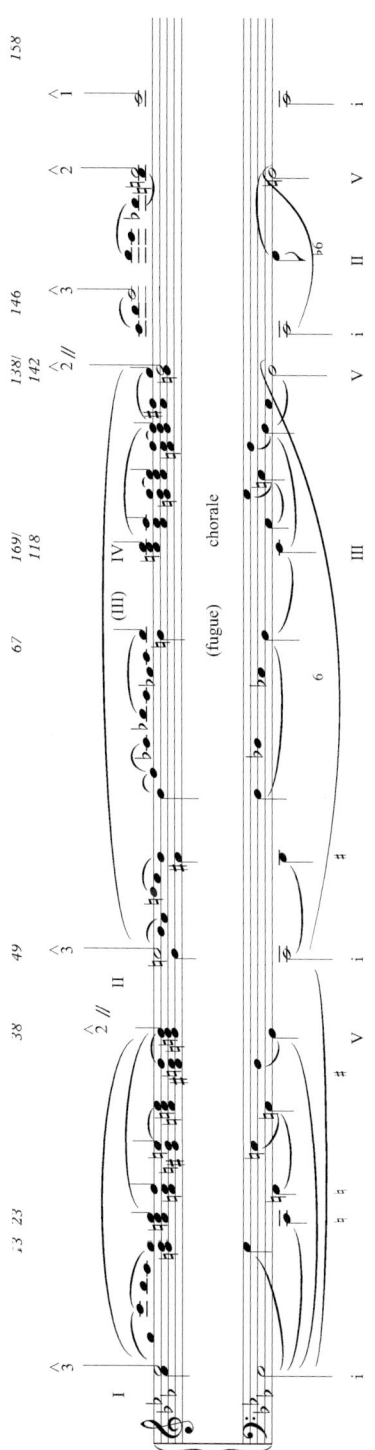

Example 3-18. Brahms (III): Middleground graph of the scherzo

Trio

We have observed in the scherzo Brahms's careful use of motives as a means of linking diverse ideas, so it seems only natural that the main theme of the trio is related to the chorale, as demonstrated in Example 3-19. The chorale begins from G5, while the trio theme leads to it, but both then descend in similar rhythmic fashion a fourth to D5, which, you may recall, is a transposition of motive x from the beginning of the scherzo. The structural difference between the themes is that the descend in the trio is to an inner voice below the prolongation of G5 by its upper neighbor, also a feature of the chorale.

The trio has a formal design a-a'-b-a", and Example 3-20 provides a graph of each of these sections. The top system is an interpretation of the first two phrases. Despite the emphasis given to G5, as demonstrated in the previous example, the primary tone is identified as E ($\hat{3}$), which leads to D ($\hat{2}$)/V in the ninth bar.[10] The extension of the dominant contains an unexpected motion to a B major chord. It is certainly possible this chord is there simply to add color, but this seems out of character for Brahms, who takes such great care in his compositional planning. Quite possibly this sound anticipates an emphasis on E Minor to follow, which, unlikely as that may seem in the context of F Minor, does happen in the slow introduction to and later in the fourth movement. The a phrase is then repeated an octave higher (violin 1), including statements of the B major chord within the prolongation of V.

---

10 My counting of bars does not include the two-bar pickup.

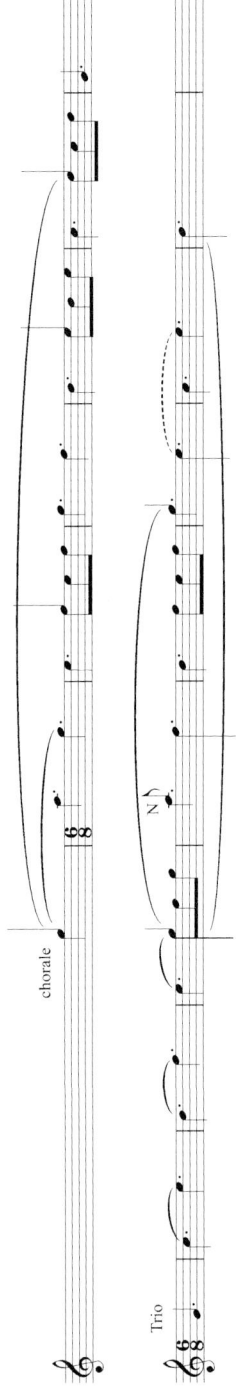

Example 3-19. Brahms (III): Comparison of chorale theme (scherzo) and trio theme

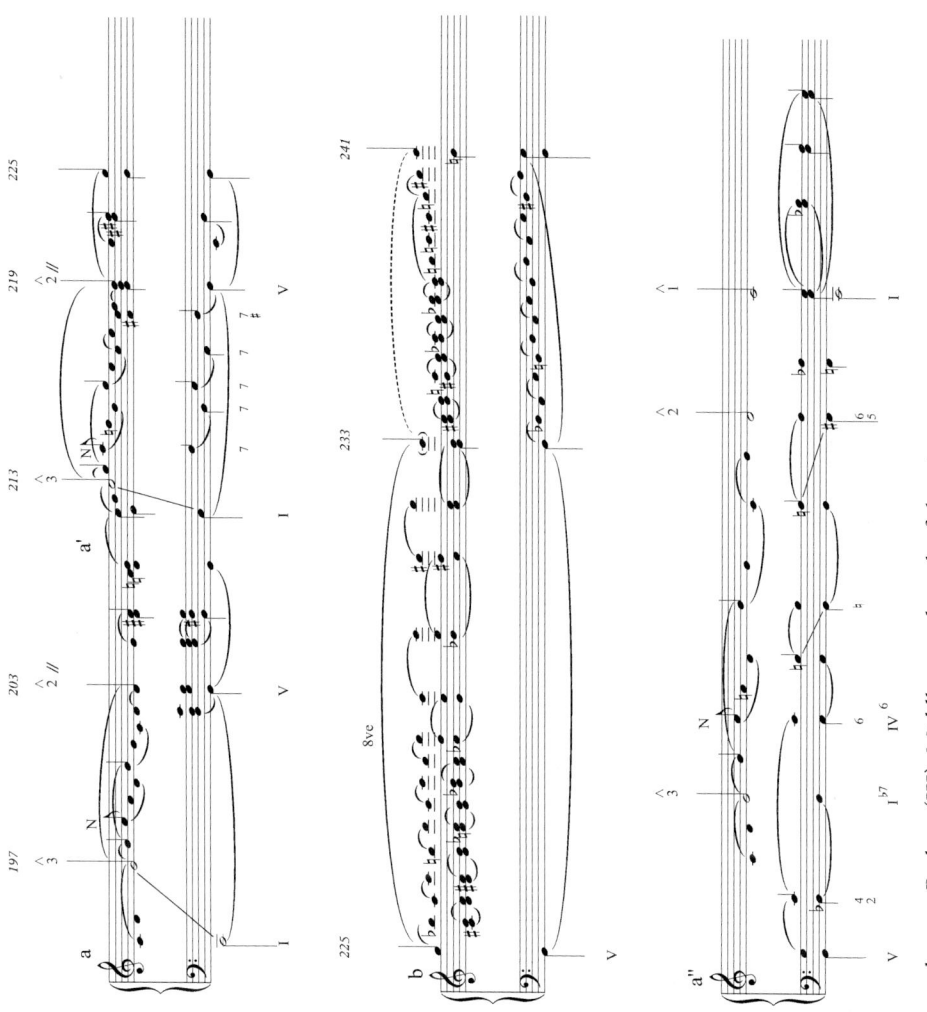

Example 3-20. Brahms (III): Middleground graph of the trio

The b section consists of two phrases. In the first the top part ascends an entire octave from G5 to G6 by the process of reaching over above a G pedal, while in the second phrase the moving parts are inverted, again sounding over a G pedal (cello). In the final phrase the melody is stated as before, however this time leading the fundamental line to closure. What is different is the harmonization, which involves a chromatic bass line that proceeds temporarily out of phase with the upper parts. The harmony emphasizes the subdominant, ending on the tonic with♭7, similar in some respects to the ending of the scherzo.

IV. Finale, poco sostenuto – allegro non troppo – presto

The ending of the scherzo is highly charged, one might even describe it as bombastic, and it also has a certain harshness to it with the concluding repeated D♭–C. So how does one proceed from there into a final movement? Brahms's solution is surprising at first, since the chromatic slow introduction is unlike anything else in the Quintet. The beginning is eerie and depressing, lacking in any clear direction, but eventually our confusion dissipates as the music wends its way to the dominant. This introduction is full of interesting references and associations that will be discussed later when we consider its voice leading in some detail. First a few comments about the formal design of the movement.

At the macro level the Finale is divided into three large sections following the slow introduction: 1) a statement of ideas (bars 41b–183); 2) a varied restatement of ideas (bars 183–342); and 3) an extended closing section / coda (bars 342–492). A closer look at the first section reveals a design very much like an exposition in sonata form. There are two statements of theme 1, the first by the cello and the second by the piano, which is followed by a passage leading to V of V. The chromatic second theme, also stated twice, is initially stated over a G pedal; it leads to an extensive transitional passage in bar 125. It is in this transition that Brahms begins to regain the momentum of the previous movement, first by changing the division of the beat into triplets, then gradually increasing the level of activity, the density, the range and the dynamic level while decreasing the span between repetitions. Having built up a head of steam, he then backs away, ending the passage with a written-out and notated *ritardando*. This leads to a charming dance-like closing section that overlaps in a clever way with the restatement of theme 1. This time the first theme is stated only once, but the continuation is greatly extended leading to the transition to theme 2. Here the second theme is initially stated over a dominant pedal in F Minor, as one would normally find in a recapitulation, and this leads to a restatement of the transitional passage, now a fifth lower, that builds as before and then recedes for a statement of the closing idea in F Minor. Essentially the movement to this point is an exposition followed directly by a recapitulation, and we can expect a coda to follow. What is unexpected is the modulation to C♯ Minor, a reference to the key of the second theme in the first movement, to initiate what is an extended section comparable in length to either of the preceding ones. This entire section, which falls into six subsections, is based in part on a motivic idea growing out of the ascending third of the opening cello theme and the chromatic second theme. It is here that Brahms finally regains the energy and drive of the previous movement. Having done so, he backs away in dramatic fashion for a brief respite – a *dolce* passage – before a final push to a powerful end featuring syncopation, very much like the dramatic close of the scherzo.

There are certain features of the slow introduction that relate back to previous movements and become prominent in this movement as well, like the opening decoration of F by G♭ (cello) and then at bar 13 the prominent D♭, the ninth of the dominant. Both pitches are also prominent here in the subsequent prolongation of V⁹, for example the restatement of the bass note C several times by D♭ in bars 31–40. See Example 3-21. Brahms also manages to refer to the B major chord that had appeared suddenly as an elaboration of the dominant in the trio from the previous movement. Here it resolves twice to an E minor chord along the path to the dominant, highlighted in the graph by brackets. The subsequent prolongation of the dominant initially involves a series of seventh chords leading to the A♭7 chord in bar 25, which is transformed into V of the E minor sixth chord to which it leads at bar 29 (*ffz*). Clearly this sound holds some significance for Brahms, and, as we shall see, this is not the last reference to E minor we will encounter in this movement.

A graph of the first theme and the following transition is provided in Example 3-22. The primary tone A♭ is introduced by the ascending third F–G–A♭ that becomes an important motivic component in the movement. Though the ascending line continues on to C and beyond, it is the A♭ that is associated with the tonic. This interpretation is substantiated by the introduction of A♭ by the seventh of the dominant for the varied repeat of the theme by the piano. This time the rising thirds lead to F5 via G♭5 as the harmony leads to VI, which at a deeper level can be understood as arising from a 5–6 motion above F, as shown below the staff in Example 3-22. This motion is embedded within a preliminary descent to closure, after which the second part of the theme descends again to local closure from A natural. The following transition opens with a statement on the tonic that is subsequently repeated a fifth higher on v, introducing G5, which then descends to an implied D5 supported by the dominant in the key of the dominant. In the subsequent prolongation of this dominant, it is the lead-in to theme 2 that connects back to G5, creating the longer-range connection between A♭5/i (bar 81) and G5/VofV (bar 93).

The chromaticism of the second theme is stated within a diatonic framework, initially sounding over a G pedal, as indicated in Example 3-23. It is the second statement of the theme beginning in bar 108 that leads to an E minor chord in first inversion in bar 112, a 5–6 motion above a sustained G, and the subsequent prolongation of this chord in bars 112–120 leads to the major tonic chord at bar 125 by an answering 5–6 motion above a sustained E natural. Finally, we are able to understand how this E minor sound fits into the larger picture. The following transition is rather complex. At the macro level the local tonic is shown to be prolonged initially by a voice exchange connecting bars 125 and 147, followed by two passages that feature the prolongation of C, supported by tonic harmony in the key of the dominant, by its upper neighbor D♭, a ♭2–1 relationship.

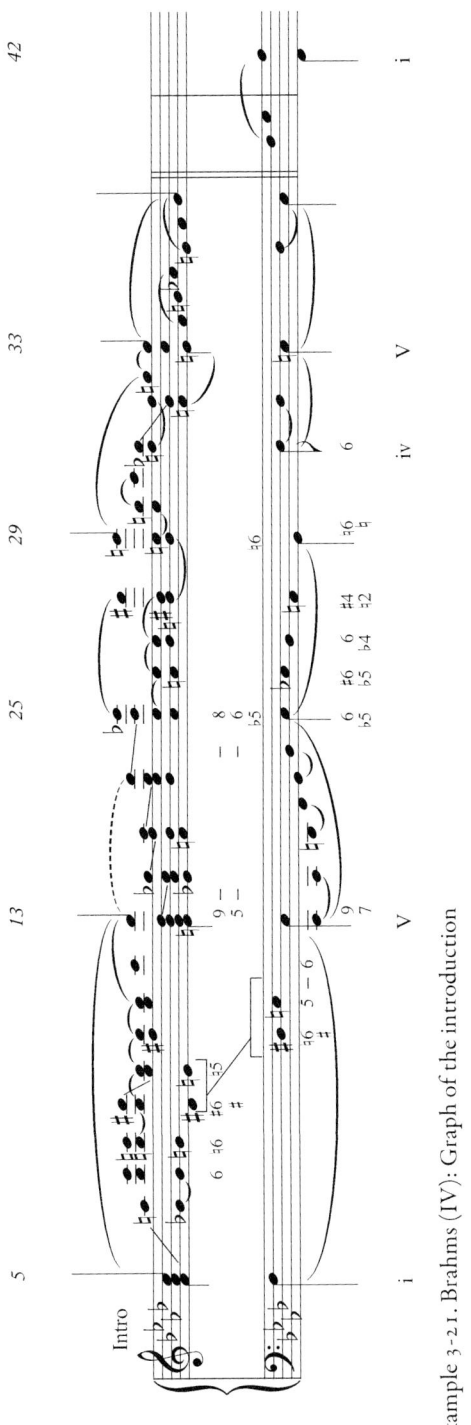

Example 3-21. Brahms (IV): Graph of the introduction

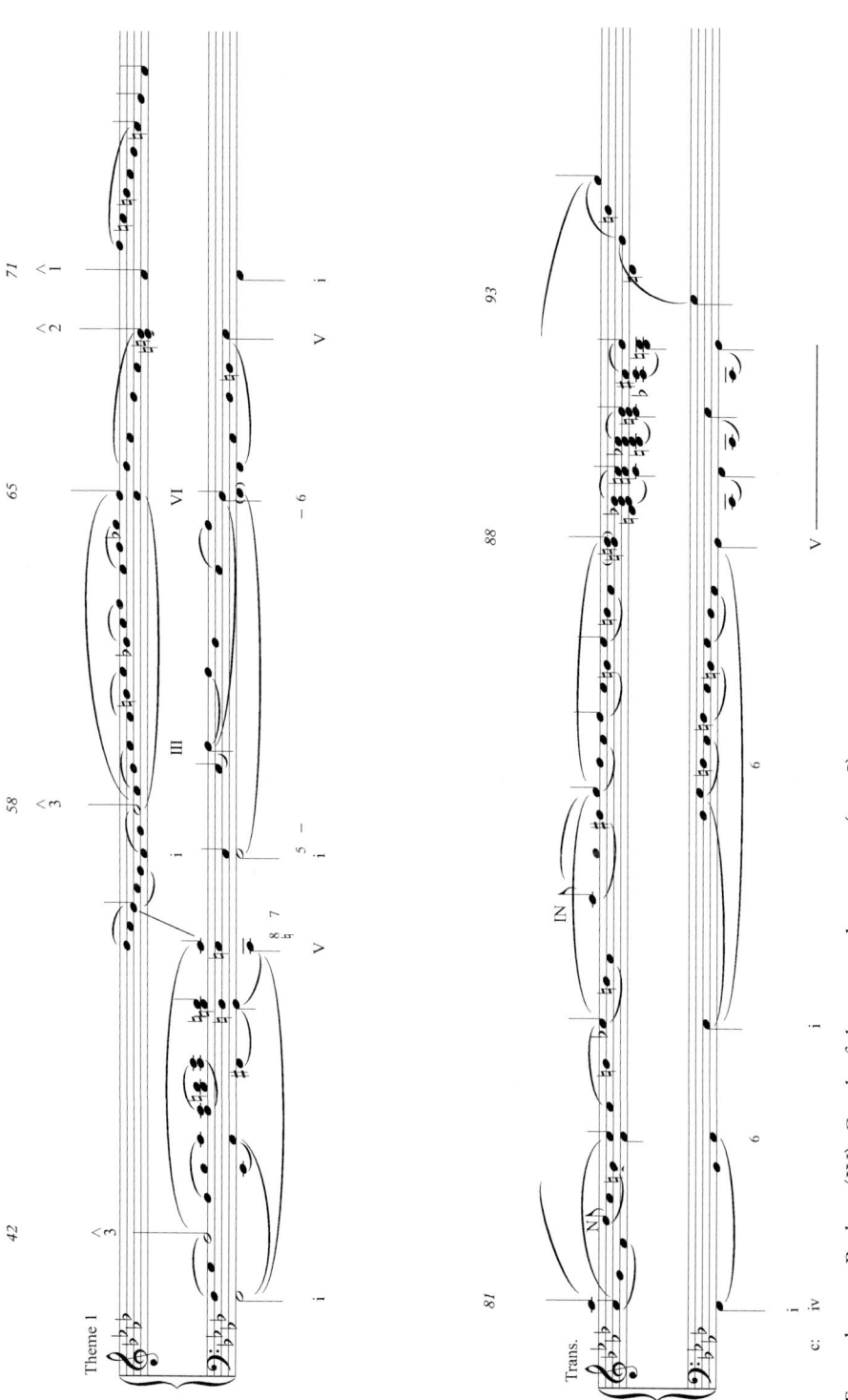

Example 3-22. Brahms (IV): Graph of theme 1 and transition (part I)

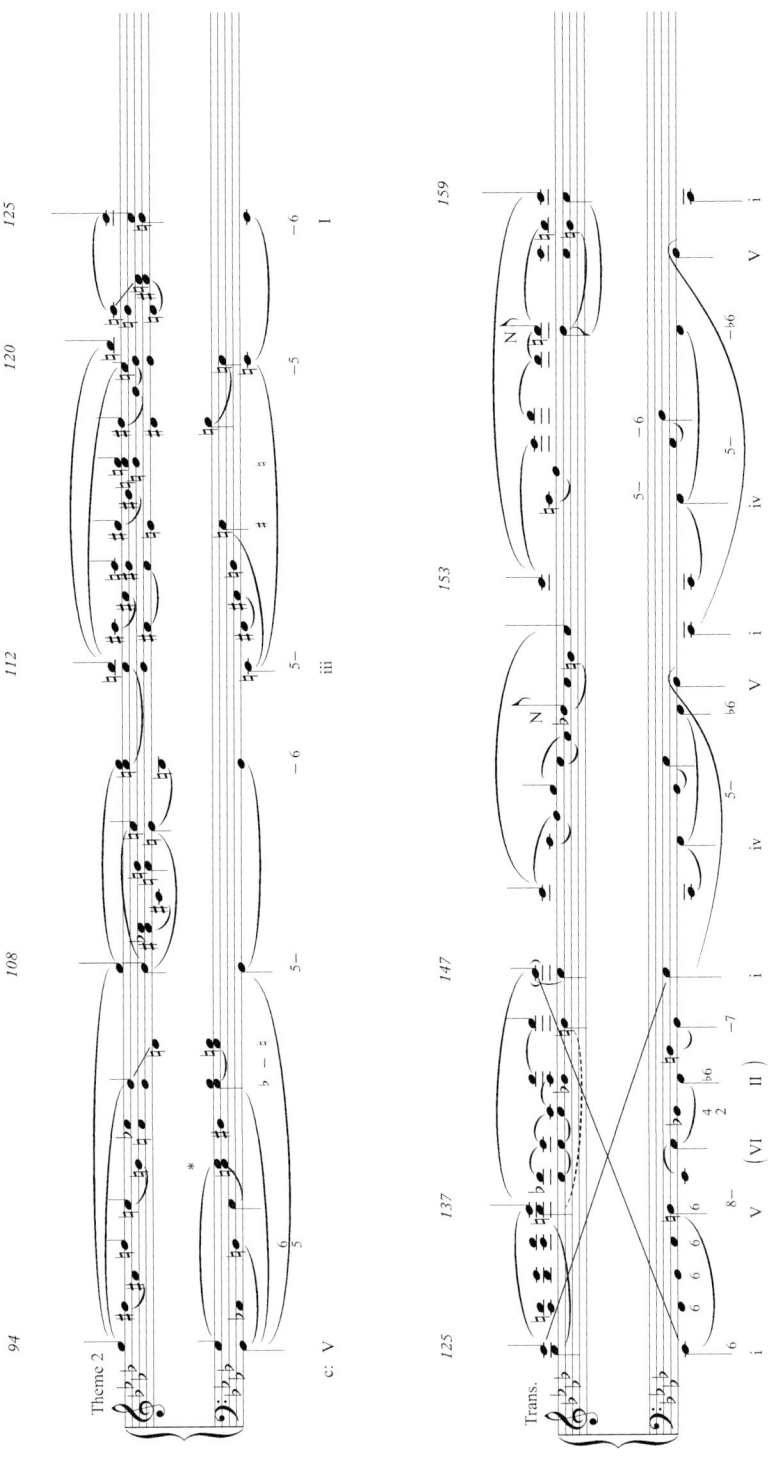

Example 3-23. Brahms (IV): Graph of theme 2 and transition (part I)

In the first part of the closing section (see Example 3-24), it is the tonic in C Minor that is prolonged, above which the melodic line reaches up to G5, then descends a fifth with a transfer to the lower octave. The repetition of this idea transforms the harmony into the dominant of F Minor above which F is shown to be suspended over V as part of the 4-3 suspension sounding in conjunction with the hesitant reintroduction of the main theme by the cello. The prolongation of G5 above is shown to be $\hat{2}$ in the interruption of the fundamental structure originating with $\hat{3}/i$ in bar 42.

The restatement opens with the first part of theme 1 stated by the cello, but the continuation is different than before. As shown in Example 3-25 by the long encompassing slur in the bass, the tonal motion across the span of theme 1 and the following transition is from i through iv (bar 239) to V (bar 246 ff.). The motion to iv involves two lower-level progressions to V, both prolonging C. The first of these, which begins from A♭ (III), is an extended dialogue between piano and strings. The second progression, which begins from a major tonic chord, initially continues this dialogue, but at bar 223 there is a progression of parallel seventh chords, where the ascending top part, running parallel to the bass, is created by the process of reaching over. [11] A covering motion then descends from E♭6 to introduce the seventh of the dominant, as if the progression were directed at A♭ and tonic harmony, but instead the harmony is re-directed to iv supporting D♭6, the upper neighbor, at the beginning of the transition. Similar to what occurred at the equivalent transition previously, this one begins with an idea that is then repeated a fifth higher reaching up to C6 and, anticipating the later statement of that pitch at bar 252, the actual point of resolution of the D♭6 from bar 234.

The statements of theme 2 and the following transition to the closing section present a single long-range tonal motion, as shown in Example 3-26, a middleground graph of bars 252–321. In this graph the statements of theme 2 are stripped of their surface chromaticism, leaving the underlying diatonic progression. The second statement (in A Minor) is shown at this level to arise from a 5–6 motion above the bass note C, which leads to a passing dominant headed to the C major chord in first inversion at bar 296, but this is delayed by the progression of parallel sixth chords initiated by the augmented sixth chord at bar 283, the beginning of the transition. Once the dominant is reached, C6, which has been prolonged since the beginning (bar 252), introduces the seventh of the dominant, resolving to A♭5 ($\hat{3}$). The remainder of the transition begins the process of leading the top sounding part toward closure, first through G♭, then G natural, but this is premature; the bass remains on C for the final four bars of the transition, reaching the tonic at the beginning of the closing section. A fully harmonized descent does follow in the lower octave in the first phrase of this closing section (not shown in the graph), but Brahms avoids a strong statement here by delaying the statement of $\hat{1}$ to introduce the varied repeat of the first phrase. This second phrase then modulates to C♯ Minor to initiate the extended coda.

---

11 The apparent parallel octaves are mitigated by intervening material not shown.

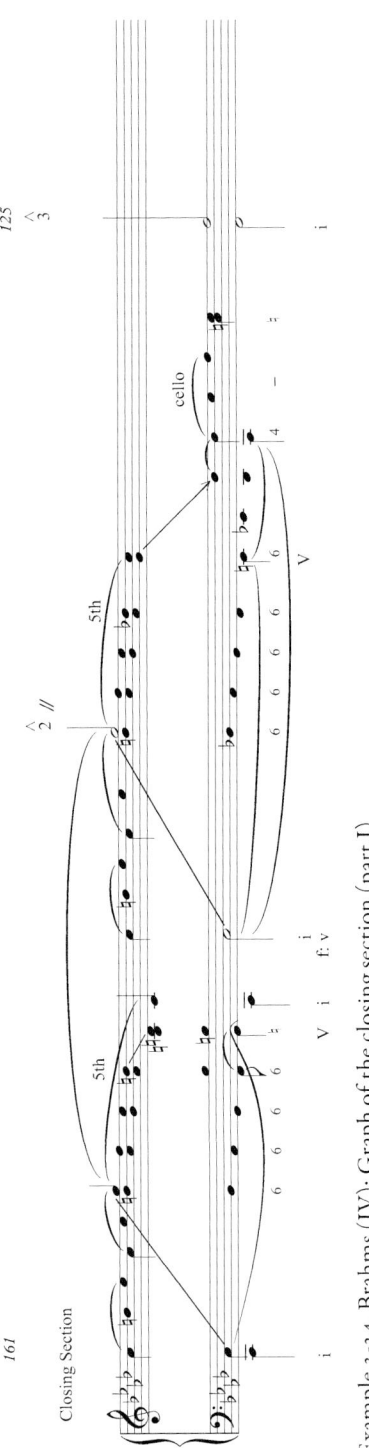

Example 3-24. Brahms (IV): Graph of the closing section (part I)

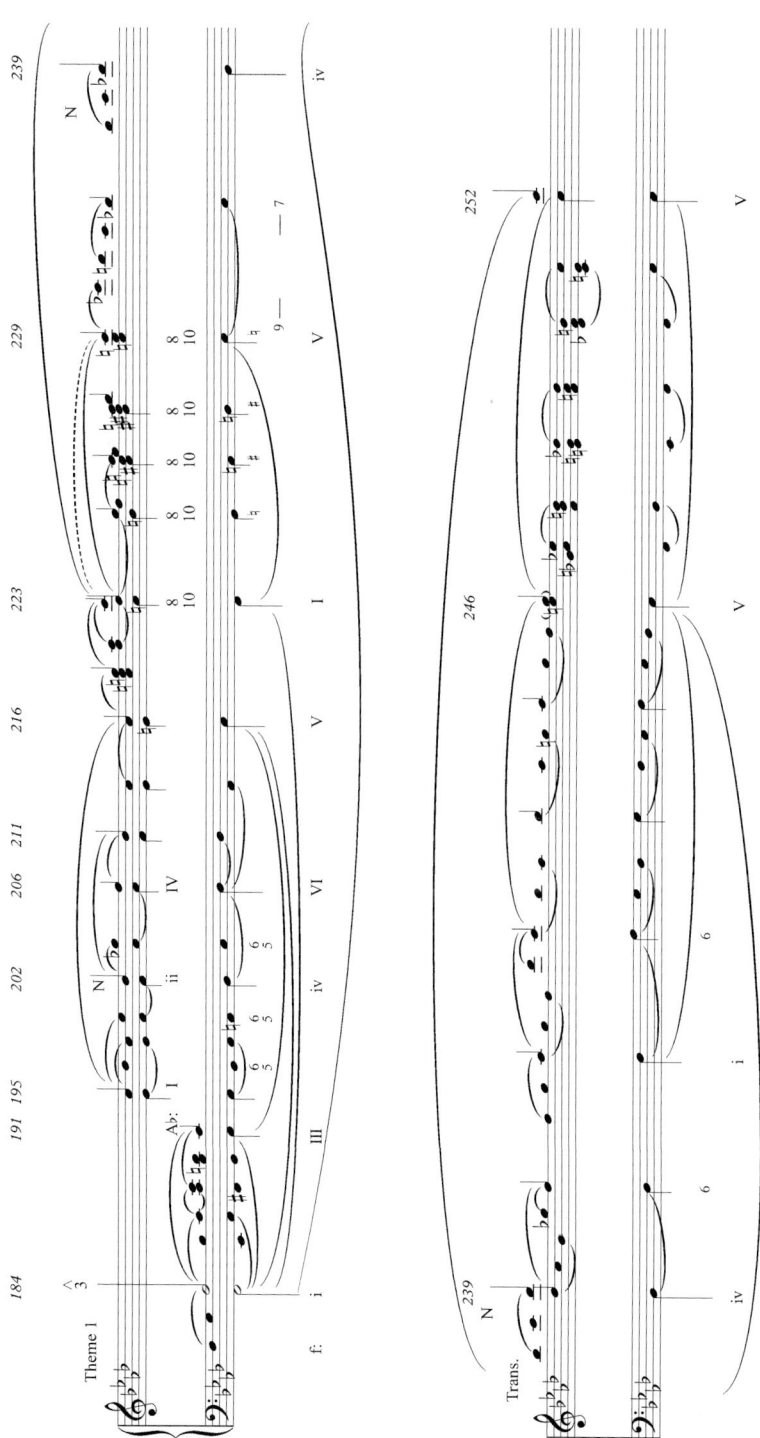

Example 3-25. Brahms (IV): Graph of theme 1 and transition (part II)

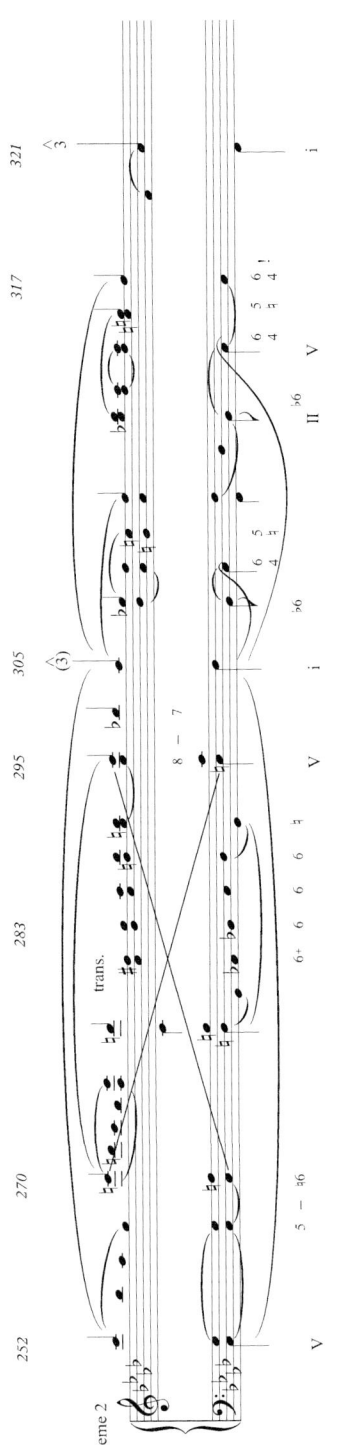

Example 3-26. Brahms (IV): Graph of theme 2 and part of the transition (part II)

It was noted previously that the coda can be divided into six sections, which now will be grouped into 2+2+1+1 based primarily on motivic/thematic content. The first two, bars 342–371 and 371–393, are based on what will be referred to as the motto, an idea that grows out of the rising third of theme 1. Its basic form in F Minor is: F–G–A♭–G–F, A♭–B♭–C–D–C. By bar 371 the dynamic level has increased from p to ff, which is retained through the second section. The next two sections, bars 394–423 and 423–439, feature theme 2, though vestiges of the motto idea continue in the accompaniment. The dynamic level remains high, and section 4 ends suddenly on a B major chord in bar 439, one final reference to E Minor without actually stating it. What does follow is a sudden break from the intensity built up over the previous sections. This fifth section, marked *tranquillo* and *dolce*, combines the motto idea and theme 2. The final section, bars 467–492 is characterized by the pervasive syncopation. It begins softly but builds gradually to the final cadence.

Example 3-27 is a middleground graph of sections 1 and 2. The voice leading of section 1 is a descent from E5 (=F♭5) to A♭4 ($\hat{3}$) progressing in parallel tenths with the bass and supported by the harmonic progression vi...iiV⁷i. Following the subsequent prolongation of A♭4/i this descent continues to F4 in the piano part, but this arrival at $\hat{1}$ is covered by the violin 1 part, which ascends to F6 (shown in the graph as F5) over the remainder of the phrase.

The initial statement of theme 2 in section 3 descends from F6 to C6, a motion embedded within the step connection from F6 to E♭6/C (bar 404), which initiates a series of ascending parallel tenths with the bass to G6/E natural, which continues to A♭6/C, a six-three chord replacing the standard six-four. The large slurs in the top voice and bass show this as the long-range goal from the beginning of this section. What follows is a resolution of 6 to 5 (A♭5 to G5, where G5 is covered by C6), which continues on to F4/i, indicated in Example 3-28 as a preliminary motion to closure that has been spread over a two-octave descent. Part 4 begins from F4/i and the top voice then arpeggiates through A♭4 to F5 over tonic harmony, which is followed by the motion to the B major chord that brings this section to an abrupt end. It seems Brahms is headed once again to E Minor, but suddenly changes his mind. The V-like symbol at this point in the graph indicates that the continuation is omitted. Instead, the next section (*tranquillo*, *dolce*) redirects the harmony to V⁷, which is prolonged through the remainder of the section.

The final section begins from a low register and dynamic level and builds gradually to bar 478. This six-four resolves to five-three in the next bar, but, as indicated in Example 3-29, this resolution is internal to a larger motion, where the top voice descends chromatically to C6/V, which leads to A♭5 and tonic harmony in bar 481. The following chromatic progression, which incorporates reference to both G♭–F and then D♭–C in the bass, leads to closure in the piano part at bar 485 an octave higher than notated in the graph. Since this motion to closure occurs in conjunction with the continuing syncopations that pervade this final section, the music must proceed until there is a strong statement of V to i on successive downbeats, which follows directly. The final melodic gesture (strings)

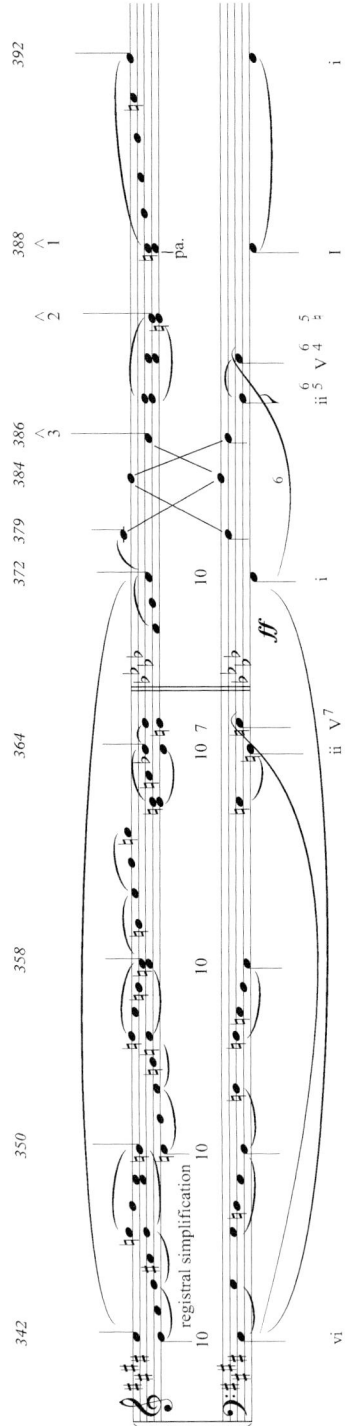

Example 3-27. Brahms (IV): Graph of bars 342–392 (part III)

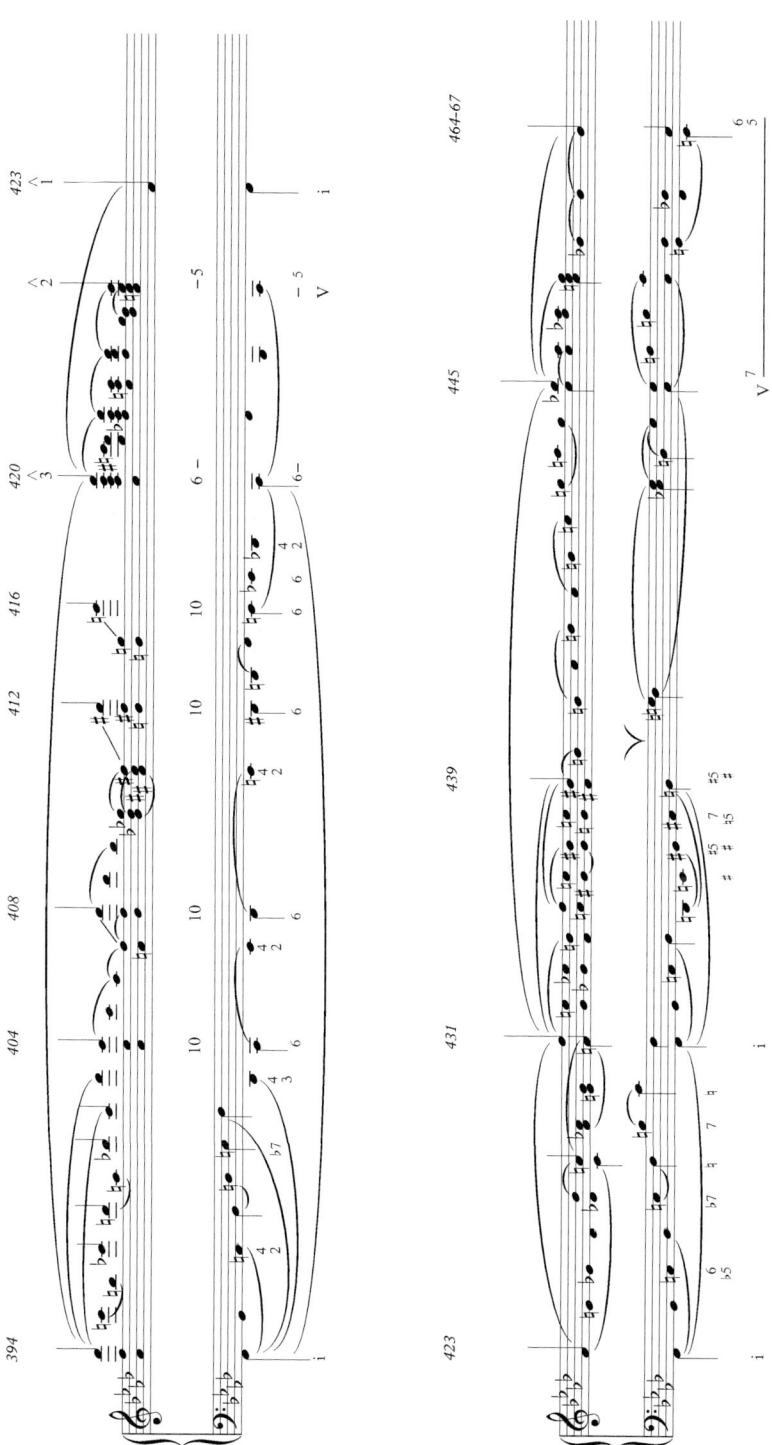

Example 3-28. Brahms (IV): Graph of bars 394–467 (part III)

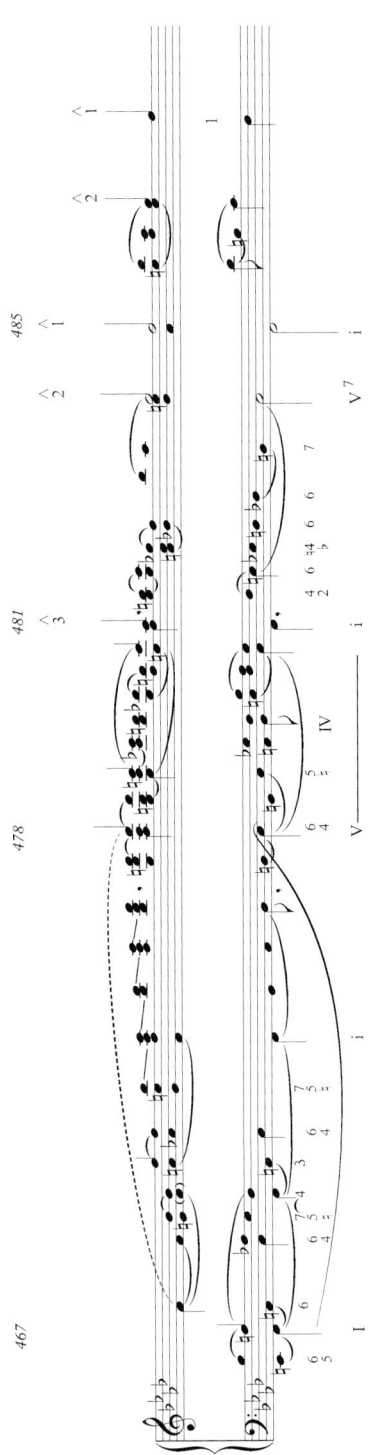

Example 3-29. Brahms (IV): Graph of bars 467–485 (part III)

ends with A♭–G–F, as if to erase all the previous statements of the rising thirds F–G–A♭ to signal the musical journey is finished.

*

This quintet presents us with several interesting analytical issues, some of which have been addressed in the preceding analysis. One question that remains unanswered is the meaning of the B7 chord and the reference to E minor. When we hear the B7 chord in the trio of the third movement, it is heard as an elaboration of the dominant: G–B7–G7. Having introduced this sound, Brahms then refers directly to E minor in the Finale, first in the slow chromatic introduction, then later cleverly worked into the second statement of theme 2 as the connective between V and I^6 in the key of the dominant (see example 3-23). This seems to provide a rationale for E minor within the context of F minor, but then we encounter a B major chord again at bar 439, which is followed directly by G7 (V of the dominant), recalling the sound juxtaposition first heard in the trio. What is Brahms referring to? Though we will never know the answer, it is interesting to consider the possibilities. One is that he is making direct reference to the Cello Sonata in E Minor, op. 38, the composition of which overlaps with that of the quintet. Another intriguing possibility is that he is referring to a progression in the fourth movement of the Schumann Quintet where a D♯7 is interjected into an area controlled by B7, anticipating the opening key of the recapitulation. See example 2-14. Though the pitch level is different, the sound is that of major triads/seventh chords a third apart: B7–G♯7–B7 (Schumann) and G–B7–G7 (Brahms). One could imagine Brahms thinking: "Here is an interesting sound I hear in the Schumann piece. Now what can *I* do with it?"

Sources consulted

Brown, Julie Hedges. "Schumann and the *style hongrois*," *Rethinking Schumann*, ed. Roh-Min Koh and Laura Tunbridge (Oxford University Press, 2011).

Caplin, William. *Classical Form: A Theory of Formal Functions for the Instrumental Music of Haydn, Mozart, and Beethoven* (Oxford University Press, 1998).

Daverio, John. *Robert Schumann: Herald of a "New Poetic Age"* (Oxford University Press, 1997).

—. *Crossing Paths: Schubert, Schumann and Brahms* (Oxford University Press, 2002).

Elvers, R., ed. *Felix Mendelssohn: A Life in Letters*, trans. C. Tomlinson (Fromm International, 1986).

Hepokoski, James and Warren Darcy. *Elements of Sonata Theory: Norms, Types and Deformation in the late Eighteenth-Century Sonata* (Oxford University Press, 2006).

Musgrave, Michael, ed. *The Cambridge Companion to Brahms* (Cambridge University Press, 1999).

—. *The Music of Brahms* (Clarendon / Oxford University Press, 1994).

Rapoport, Erez. *The Smoothing Over of Formal Junctures as a Style Element in Mendelssohn's Instrumental Music* (Dissertation: CUNY Graduate Center, 2004).

Smith, Peter. "Associative Harmony, Tonal Pairing and Middleground Structures in Schumann's Expositions," *Rethinking Schumann*, ed. Roh-Min Koh and Laura Tunbridge (Oxford University Press, 2011).

Todd, R. Larry. *Fanny Hensel: The Other Mendelssohn* (Oxford University Press, 2010).

—. *Mendelssohn: A Life in Music* (Oxford University Press, 2003).

—. *Mendelssohn Essays* (Routledge, 2008).

Wollenberg, Susan. "Schumann's Piano Quintet in E flat: The Bach Legacy," *The Music Review* 52/4 (November 1991).